SUMMER BRAIN QUEST

Dear Parents and Educators,

At Brain Quest, we believe learning should be an adventure—a *quest* for knowledge. Our mission has always been to guide children on that quest, to keep them excited, motivated, and curious, and to give them the confidence they need to do well in school. Now, we're extending the adventure to summer vacation! Meet SUMMER BRAIN QUEST: It's a workbook. It's a game. It's an outdoor adventure. And it's going to stop summer slide!

Research shows that if kids take a break from learning all summer, they can lose up to three months' worth of knowledge from the previous grade. So we set out to create a one-of-a-kind workbook experience that delivers personalized learning for every kind of kid. Personalized learning is an educational method where exercises are tailored to each child's strengths, needs, and interests. Our goal was to empower kids to have a voice in what and how they learned during the summer, while ensuring they get enough practice with the fundamentals they need. The result: SUMMER BRAIN QUEST—a complete interactive program that is easy to use and designed to engage each unique kid all summer long.

So how does it work? Each SUMMER BRAIN QUEST WORKBOOK includes a pullout tri-fold map that functions as a game board, progress chart, and personalized learning system. Our map corresponds to 110 pages of curriculum-based exercises and 8 outdoor learning experiences. We've also included over 160 stickers to mark progress, incentivize challenging exercises, and celebrate accomplishments. As kids complete activities and earn stickers, they can put them wherever they like on the map, so each child's map is truly unique—just like each kid. To top it all off, we included a Summer Brainiac Award Certificate to mark your child's successful completion of the quest. SUMMER BRAIN QUEST guides kids so they feel supported, and it offers positive feedback and builds confidence by showing kids how far they've come, what they have learned, and just how much they've accomplished.

Each SUMMER BRAIN QUEST WORKBOOK has been created in consultation with an award-winning teacher specializing in that grade. We cover the core competencies of reading, writing, and math, as well as the essentials of social studies and science. We ensure our exercises are aligned to Common Core State Standards, Next Generation Science Standards, and state social studies standards.

Loved by kids and adored by teachers, Brain Quest is America's #1 educational bestseller and has been an important bridge to the classroom for millions of children. SUMMER BRAIN QUEST is an effective new tool for parents, homeschoolers, tutors, and teachers alike to stop summer slide. By providing fun, personalized, and meaningful educational materials, our mission is to help ALL kids keep their skills ALL summer long. We want kids to know:

It's your summer. It's your workbook. It's your learning adventure.

—The editors of Brain Quest

This book belongs to:

Workman Kids
Workman Publishing
Hachette Book Group, Inc.
1290 Avenue of the Americas
New York, NY 10104
workman.com

Workman Kids is an imprint of Workman Publishing, a division of Hachette Book Group, Inc. BRAIN QUEST, IT'S FUN TO BE SMART!, and the Workman name and logo are registered trademarks of Hachette Book Group, Inc.

Summer Series Concept by Nathalie Le Du, Daniel Nayeri, Tim Hall
Writer   Bridget Heos
Consulting Editor   Kimberly Oliver Burnim
Art Director   Colleen AF Venable
Cover, Map, Sticker, and Additional Character Illustrator   Edison Yan
Illustrator   Maris Wicks
Series Designer   Tim Hall
Editor   Carol M. Burrell
Production Editor   Jessica Rozler
Production Manager   Julie Primavera

Workman books may be purchased in bulk for business, educational, or promotional use. For information, please contact your local bookseller or the Hachette Book Group Special Markets Department at special.markets@hbgusa.com.

Library of Congress Cataloging-in-Publication Data is available.

ISBN 978-1-5235-0299-8

First Edition March 2018 APS

Distributed in Europe by Hachette Livre, 58 rue Jean Bleuzen, 92 178 Vanves Cedex, France.

Distributed in the United Kingdom by Hachette Book Group, UK, Carmelite House, 50 Victoria Embankment, London EC4Y 0DZ.

Printed in China on responsibly sourced paper.

10 9 8

BETWEEN GRADES
Pre-K&K

For adventurers ages 4–5

Written by Bridget Heos

Consulting Editor: Kimberly Oliver Burnim

WORKMAN PUBLISHING

NEW YORK

4

Contents

Your Quest

Your quest is to sticker as many paths on the map as possible and reach the final destination by the end of summer to become an official Summer Brainiac.

Basic Components

Summer progress map

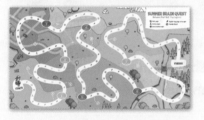

100+ pages of quest exercises

110 quest stickers

8 Outside Quests

8 Outside Quest stickers

Over 40 achievement stickers

Summer Brainiac Award

100% sticker

Setup

Detach the map and place it on a flat surface.

Begin at **START** on your map.

How to Play

To advance along a path, you must complete a quest exercise with the matching color and symbol. For example:

Math exercise from the orange level (Level 2)

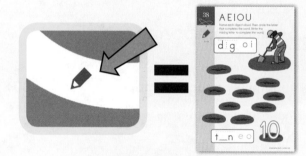

English language arts exercise from the red level (Level 3)

Social studies exercise from the purple level (Level 5)

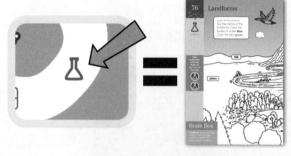

Science exercise from the blue level (Level 6)

If you complete the challenge, you earn a matching quest sticker.

Place the quest sticker on the path to continue on your journey.

At the end of each level, you earn an achievement sticker.

Apply it to the map and move on to the next level!

Outside Quests

Throughout the map, you will encounter paths that lead to Outside Quests.

To advance along those paths, you must complete one of the Outside Quests.

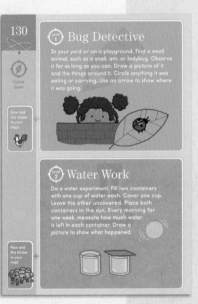

If you complete an Outside Quest, you earn an Outside Quest sticker and advance toward 100% completion!

Bonuses

If you complete a bonus question, you earn an achievement sticker.

BONUS: How many flies are there? Write the number. → **Now add this sticker to your map!**

Subject Completion

If you complete all of the quest exercises in a subject (math, English language arts, science, or social studies), you earn an achievement sticker.

CONGRATULATIONS! You completed all of your science quests! You earned:

Summer Brain Quest Completion Sticker and Award

If you complete your quest, you earn a Summer Brain Quest completion sticker and award!

100% Sticker

Sticker *every* possible route and finish *all* the Outside Quests to earn the 100% sticker!

Level
1

ABCs

Your Name

Circle the first letter of your first name in uppercase. Then underline the lowercase letters that are in your first name.

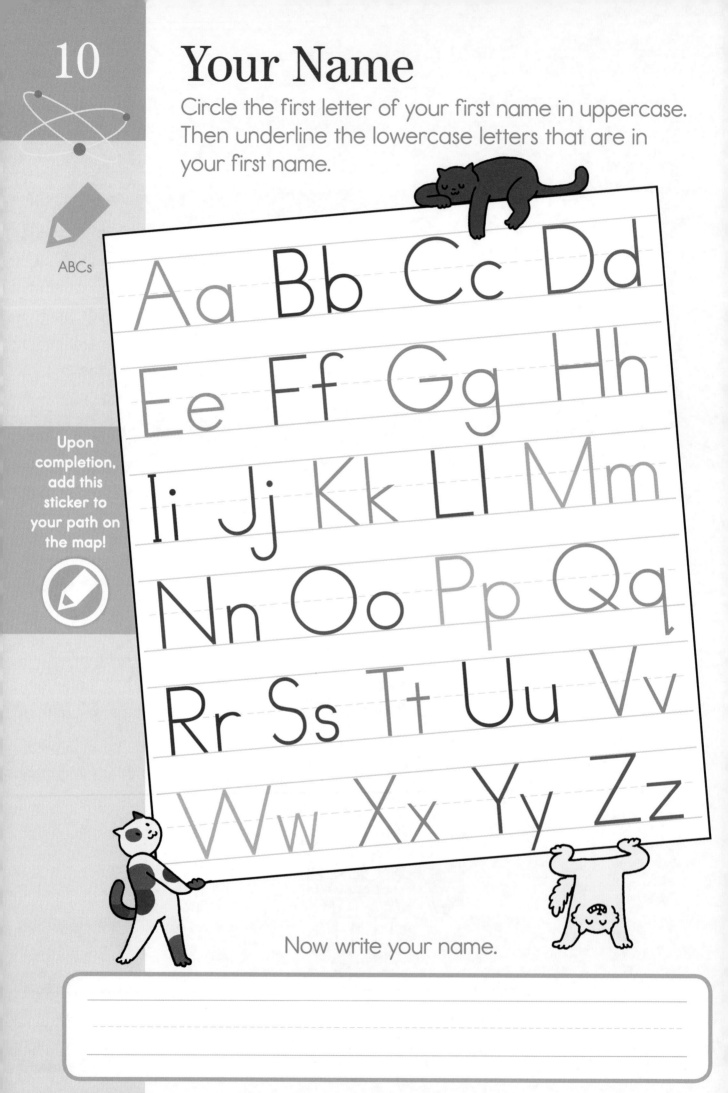

Aa Bb Cc Dd
Ee Ff Gg Hh
Ii Jj Kk Ll Mm
Nn Oo Pp Qq
Rr Ss Tt Uu Vv
Ww Xx Yy Zz

Now write your name.

Count

Count the items in each set.
Then trace the number.

11

Numbers: 1–5

1 firetruck

2 firefighters

3 trees

4 cats

5 children

Upon completion, add this sticker to your path on the map!

12

My World

My Family

Look at each activity. Circle one activity you like to do with your family.

Upon completion, add this sticker to your path on the map!

Draw a picture of your family doing your favorite activity.

The Five Senses

Draw a line from the picture to the sense that goes best with it.

Senses

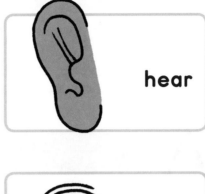

hear

see

Upon completion, add this sticker to your path on the map!

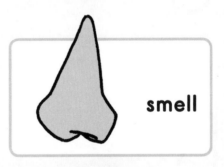

smell

touch

taste

Brain Box

You use your senses to hear, see, smell, touch, and taste things.

A B C D E F

Trace the uppercase and lowercase letters.
Then write the uppercase and lowercase letters.
Say the name of the object that begins with
that letter.

Upon
completion,
add these
stickers to
your path on
the map!

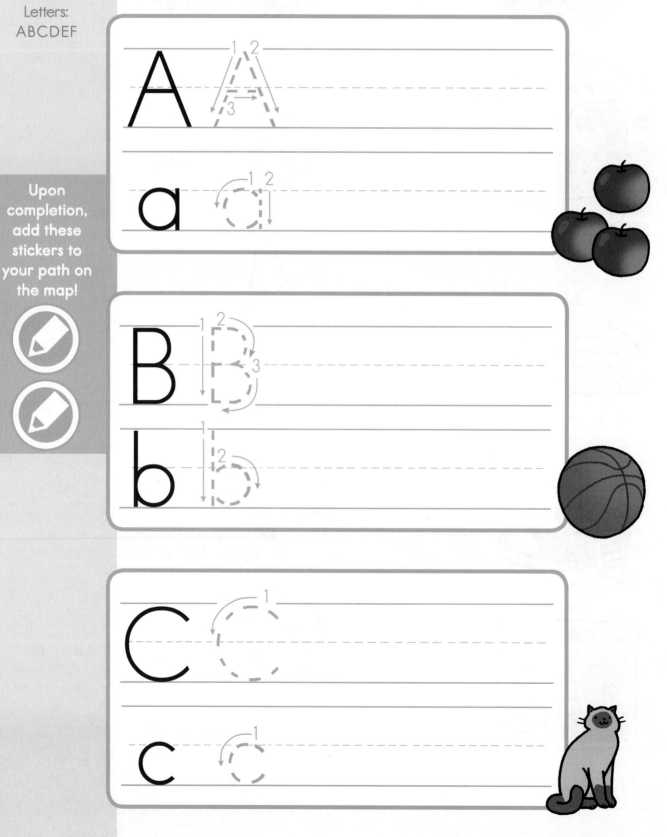

D d

E e

F f

Letters:
ABCDEF

BONUS:
Draw
something
that starts
with the
letter b.

Now add
this sticker
to your
map!

Colors

Upon completion, add these stickers to your path on the map!

Cat-astrophe!

Look at the neighborhood. Follow the directions to color the picture.

Colors

Color the firetruck **red**.
Color the cat **orange**.
Color the bird **blue**.
Color the dog walker's shirt **purple**.
Color the tree trunk **brown**.
Color the leaves and grass **green**.
Color the house yellow.
Color the kids **all different** colors.

BONUS: What color comes from mixing red and blue? Color the doghouse that color.

Now add this sticker to your map!

G H I

Trace the uppercase and lowercase letters.
Then write the uppercase and lowercase letters.
Say the name of the object that begins with
that letter.

Upon
completion,
add this
sticker to
your path on
the map!

Level 1 complete!

Add this achievement sticker to your path…

…and move on to

Level 2!

J K L

Trace the uppercase and lowercase letters. Then write the uppercase and lowercase letters. Say the name of the object that begins with that letter.

Letters: J K L

Upon completion, add this sticker to your path on the map!

Farm to Market

Read about the workers. Then follow the directions.

The **farmer** grows the wheat.
Draw a line under the farmer.

The **miller** grinds the wheat into flour.
Draw a circle around the miller.

The **baker** uses the flour to bake bread.
Draw a triangle around the baker.

The **grocer** sells the bread at her store.
Draw a square around the grocer.

Community

Upon completion, add this sticker to your path on the map!

Count the number of each type of animal in the watermelon patch. Find the box with the name of that animal. Then trace the number.

Counting

Upon completion, add these stickers to your path on the map!

BONUS: How many flies are there? Write the number.

flies

Now add this sticker to your map!

MNO

Trace the uppercase and lowercase letters.
Then write the uppercase and lowercase letters.
Say the name of the object that begins with
that letter.

Letters: M N O

Upon
completion,
add this
sticker to
your path on
the map!

Lunch Time!

Look at the map of the farm. Start at the pond and draw a line along the path to the farmhouse.

Upon completion, add this sticker to your path on the map!

BONUS: Bees make honey and live in beehives. Find the beehive on the map and circle it.

Now add this sticker to your map!

P Q R S T

Trace the uppercase and lowercase letters.
Then write the uppercase and lowercase letters.
Say the name of the object that begins with
that letter.

Upon
completion,
add these
stickers to
your path on
the map!

Letters:
PQRST

R R

r r

S S

s s

T T

t t

BONUS: What letter are the chicks forming?

Now add this sticker to your map!

Fun Shapes

Shapes

Upon completion, add these stickers to your path on the map!

Trace the circle. Then draw your own circle. Color your circle **orange**, like an orange.

Trace the triangle. Then draw your own triangle. Color your triangle yellow, like a slice of cheese.

SNIFF SNIFF

Trace the rectangle. Then draw your own rectangle. Make your rectangle into a garden by coloring it **green**.

Trace the square. Then draw your own square. Make your square into a pool by coloring it **blue**.

My Plant and Me

Draw a line from the child to the things she needs.
Draw a line from the plant to the things it needs.
(**Hint:** There are two things that both plants and people need.)

Brain Box

People and plants are living things. But a person and plant need different things to grow.

Level 2 complete!

Add this achievement sticker
to your path...

...and move on to
Level
3!

Community

Look at the picture. Color the things that keep people safe.

Upon completion, add this sticker to your path on the map!

Color the hard hats yellow. They protect the workers' heads.

Color the goggles **gray**. They protect the workers' eyes.

Color the gloves **red**. They protect the workers' hands.

Color the cones **orange**. They keep other people out of the construction zone.

Tool Time

Look at the pictures. Circle the tool that would help with the job.

Upon completion, add this sticker to your path on the map!

U V W X Y Z

Trace the uppercase and lowercase letters. Then write the uppercase and lowercase letters. Say the name of the object that begins with that letter.

Letters:
U V W X Y Z

WALK

Trace and write the letters. Say the name of the object that **ends** with the letter.

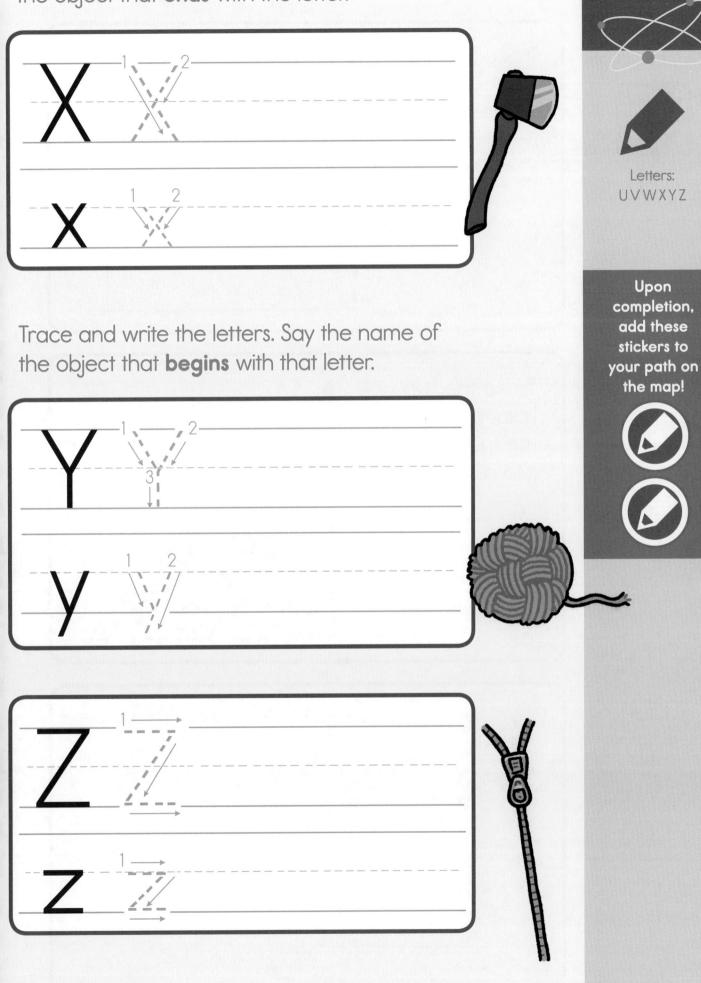

Trace and write the letters. Say the name of the object that **begins** with that letter.

Letters:
U V W X Y Z

Upon completion, add these stickers to your path on the map!

Two Shapes Together

Upon completion, add this sticker to your path on the map!

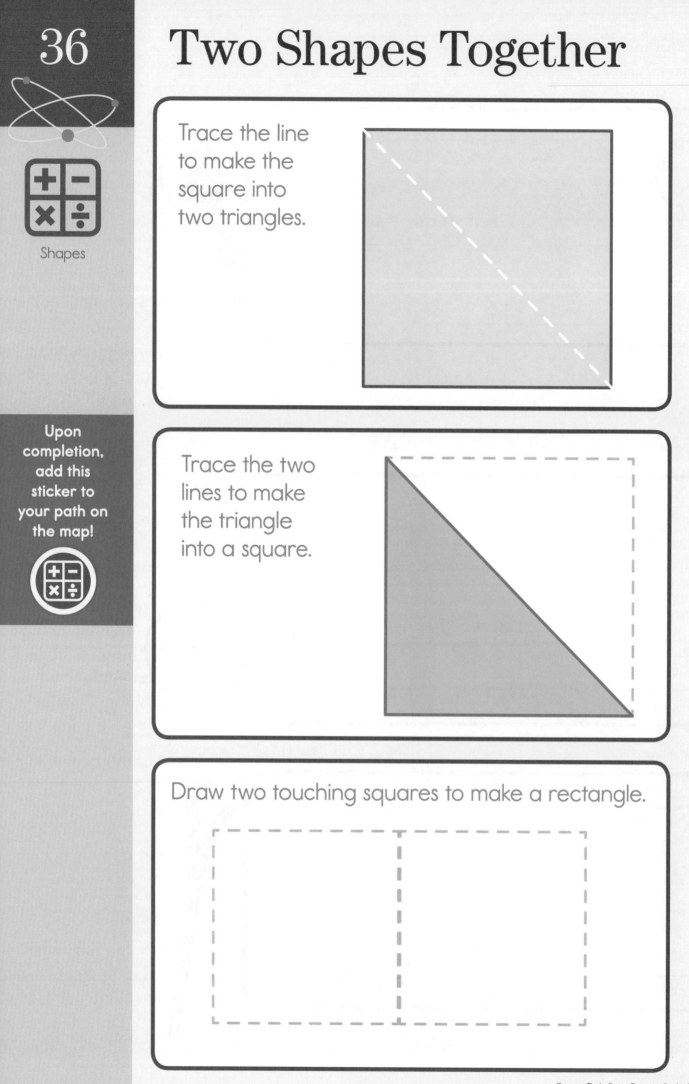

Trace the line to make the square into two triangles.

Trace the two lines to make the triangle into a square.

Draw two touching squares to make a rectangle.

Home Sweet Home

Draw a line from the animal to its habitat.

Upon completion, add this sticker to your path on the map!

Alligators eat animals, but deer eat plants.

Circle some of the things the deer might eat.

Brain Box

Animals live in different **habitats**. The habitat has food and shelter for the animal.

AEIOU

Say the word that describes the picture aloud. Then circle the letter that completes the word. Write the missing letter to complete the word.

Vowels

d_ig   o i

t_n   e o

10

Vowels

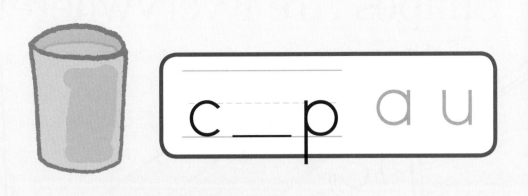

Upon completion, add these stickers to your path on the map!

BONUS: What words can you write? Write a word on the construction worker's sign.

Now add this sticker to your map!

Shapes Are Everywhere!

Look at the picture. Then follow the directions.

Shapes

Color the triangles **red**.
Color the squares **blue**.
Color the rectangles **green**.
Color the circles **orange**.
Color the stars **yellow**.
Color the hearts **pink**.

41

Shapes

Upon completion, add these stickers to your path on the map!

BONUS: The excavator will pick up oval-shaped stones. It will not pick up circle-shaped stones. Color the stones that the excavator will pick up purple.

Now add this sticker to your map!

Dive In!

The animals have taken over the construction site! Say the name of each object in the picture. What is the first sound you hear? Write the letter to complete the word.

Phonics

police officer

PIZZA

dig

elephant

dump truck

stop sign

birds

nest

Phonics

Upon completion, add these stickers to your path on the map!

New Road

Look at the pictures. Count the items in both pictures. Then write the total number.

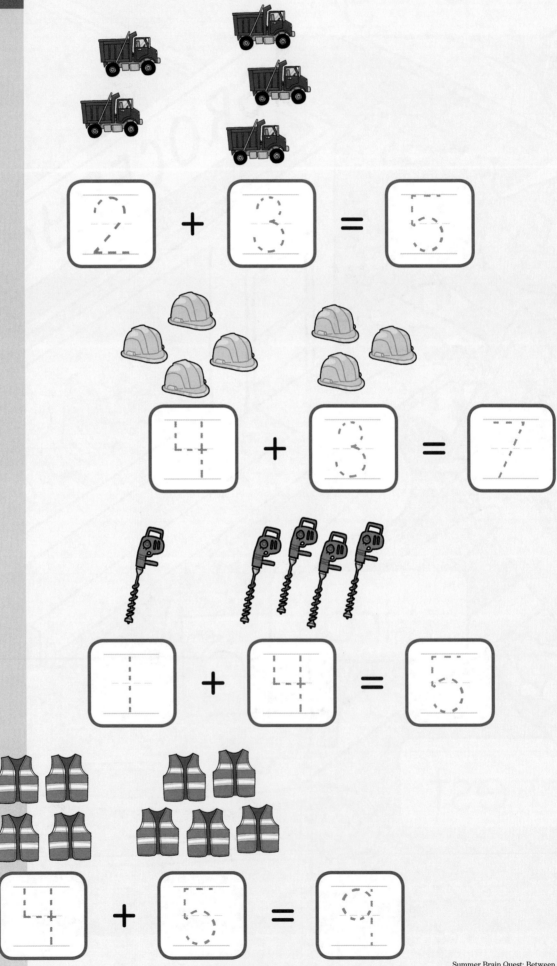

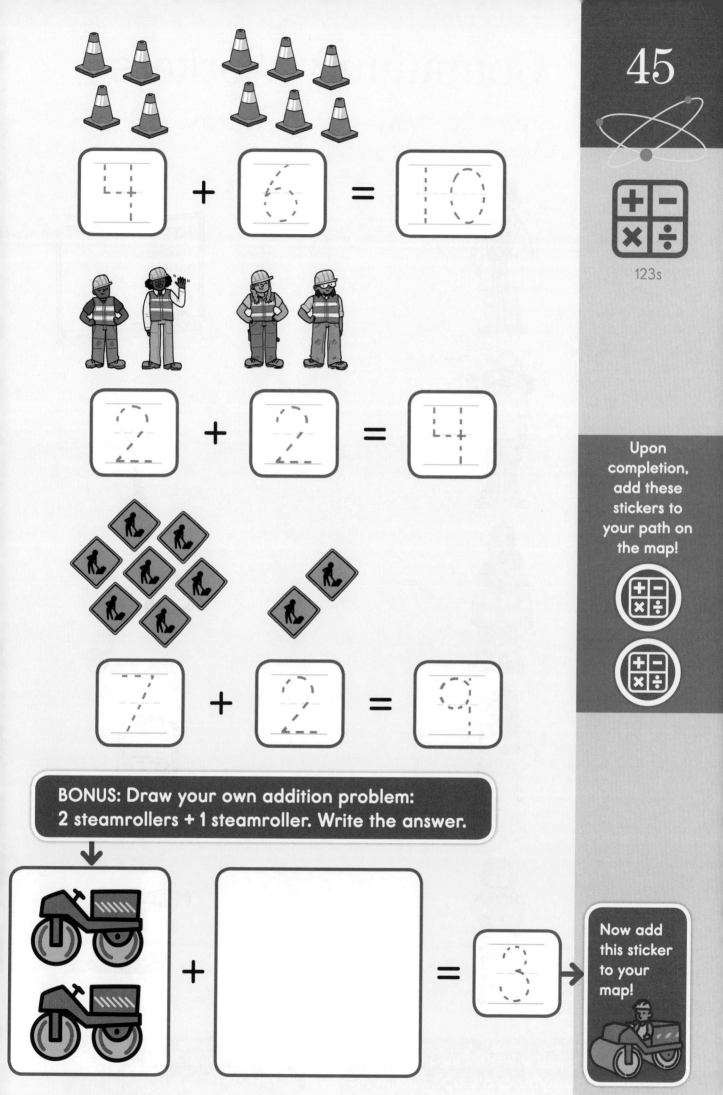

123s

$4 + 6 = 10$

$2 + 2 = 4$

$7 + 2 = 9$

Upon completion, add these stickers to your path on the map!

BONUS: Draw your own addition problem:
2 steamrollers + 1 steamroller. Write the answer.

$+ = 3$

Now add this sticker to your map!

Community

Community Workers

Draw a line from the community workers to the tools and equipment they use.

Upon completion, add this sticker to your path on the map!

TUESDAY!
• READING
• SCIENCE PROJECTS
• MATH

BONUS: Which job would you most like to have when you grow up? Circle it.

Now add this sticker to your map!

Level 3 complete!

Add this achievement sticker
to your path…

…and move on to

Level 4!

More or Less

Upon completion, add this sticker to your path on the map!

Firehouse

Circle the firefighter who has more. If the firefighters have the same number, circle them both.

Reduce, Reuse, Recycle

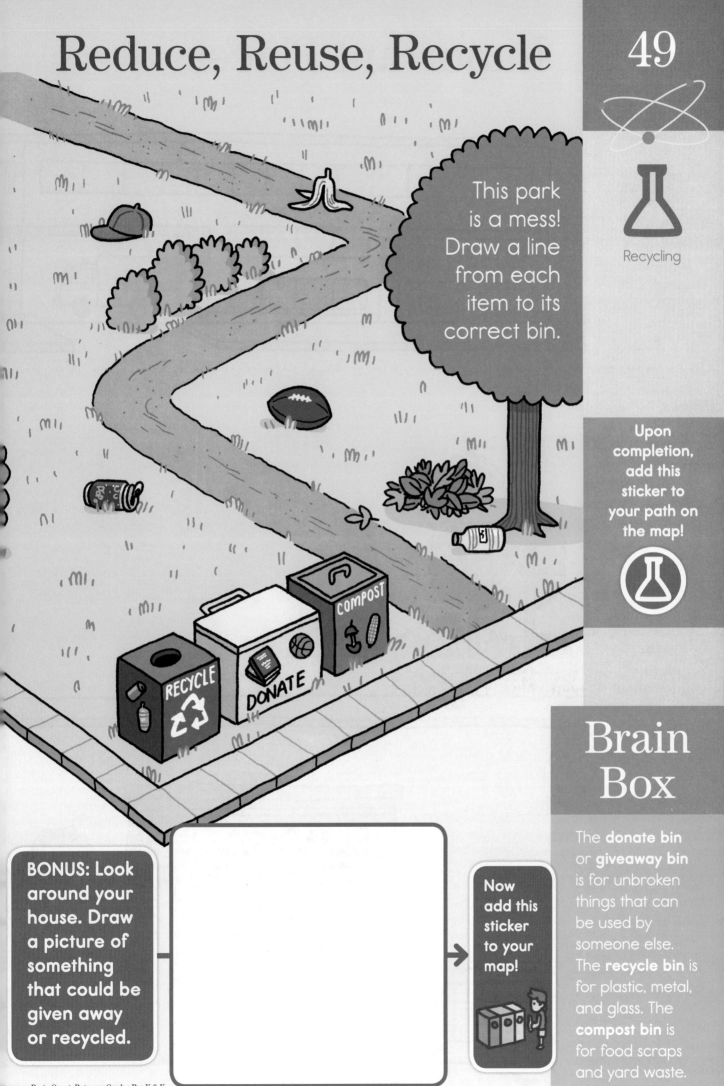

This park is a mess! Draw a line from each item to its correct bin.

Upon completion, add this sticker to your path on the map!

Brain Box

The **donate bin** or **giveaway bin** is for unbroken things that can be used by someone else. The **recycle bin** is for plastic, metal, and glass. The **compost bin** is for food scraps and yard waste.

BONUS: Look around your house. Draw a picture of something that could be given away or recycled.

Now add this sticker to your map!

Important Places

Upon completion, add these stickers to your path on the map!

Brain Box

A **library** is a place where you can read books or borrow them to take home for a while.

The community is missing somewhere important: a library! Can you draw a library in the shape of a rectangle?

POLICE

GROCERY

BONUS: If you could design a park for your community, what would it look like? Draw a picture.

Now add this sticker to your map!

Opposites at the Library

Look at each picture and say the word.
Color the picture that is its opposite.

Spelling and Vocabulary

Upon completion, add this sticker to your path on the map!

happy

sad

busy

quiet

loud

fast

full

empty

flat

tall

short

large

Opposites Around Town

Look at each picture and say the words.
Color the picture that is its opposite.

Spelling and Vocabulary

go to sleep

play

wake up

Upon completion, add this sticker to your path on the map!

push

pull

carry

sink

float

fly

count

save

spend

1...2...3...

Hospital Math

Count the objects. Then answer the questions.

There are 8 patients. 2 go home.
Cross them out. How many are left?

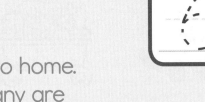

There are 6 doctors. 2 go home.
Cross them out. How many are
at work?

Subtraction

There are 6 bandages. 4 are put on patients. Cross them out. How many are left?

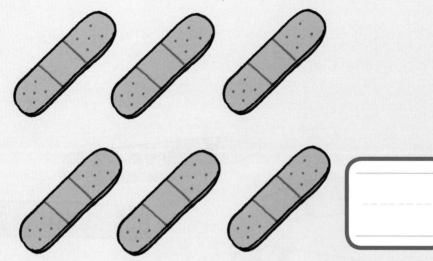

There are 5 trays of food. 2 are given to patients. Cross them out. How many are left?

Upon completion, add these stickers to your path on the map!

BONUS: Draw your own subtraction problem: Draw 4 flowers for the patients. Then cross out 2. How many are left?

Now add this sticker to your map!

Phonics

Color Rhymes

Each picture rhymes with the name of a color.
Say the word. Point to the rhyming color.
Then color the picture that color.

Level 4 complete!

Add this achievement sticker
to your path…

…and move on to

Level
5!

Phonics

Upon completion, add this sticker to your path on the map!

Main Street Rhymes

On the left are pictures from Main Street.
On the right are words that rhyme with them.
Draw a line to match the rhyming pictures.

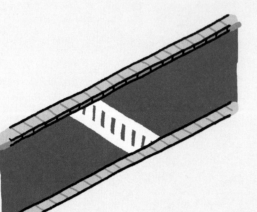

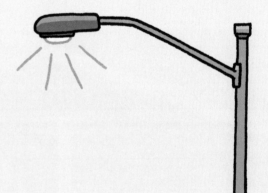

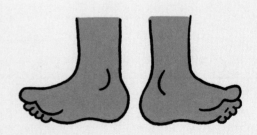

10 on the Shelf

The grocer likes to have 10 of every fruit on the shelf at her store. Draw more of each fruit to make 10.

ORANGES

APPLES

Upon completion, add this sticker to your path on the map!

CANTALOUPES

KIWIS

Weather Report

Draw a picture of the weather today.

Weather

Upon completion, add this sticker to your path on the map!

Circle the symbol that shows what the weather is like.

Circle the clothing people should wear for the weather today.

BONUS: Find out what the temperature is today. Write the number here:

_____ degrees

Now add this sticker to your map!

Yay, Day!

Imagine the best day ever. Draw pictures in the circles to show what you would do in the morning, afternoon, and night.

My World

Upon completion, add this sticker to your path on the map!

morning

afternoon

night

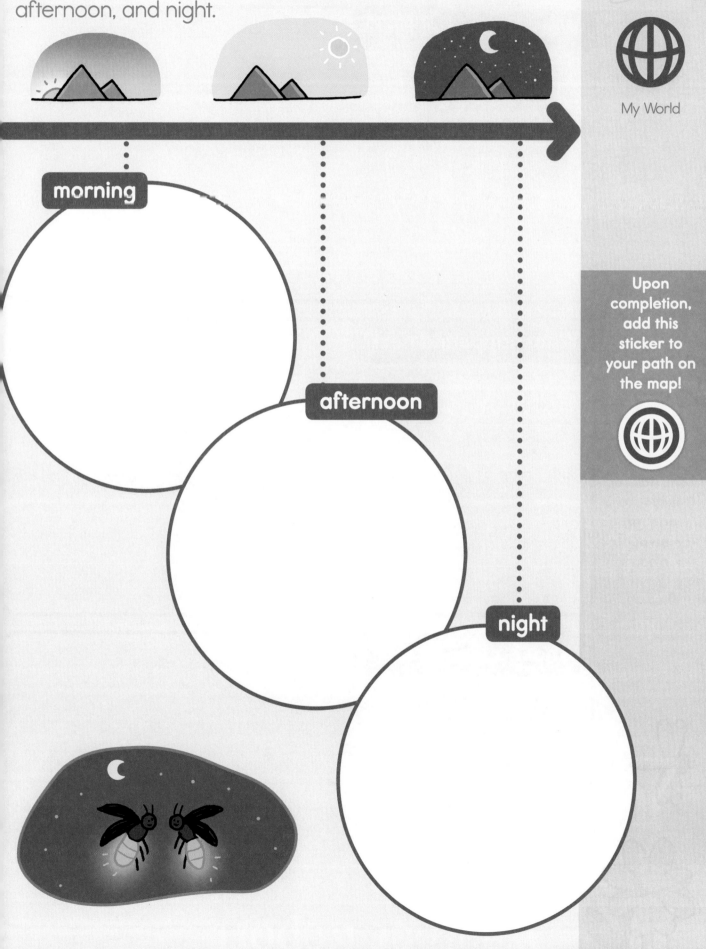

Storytelling

My Memory

What is a special memory you have from this summer? Draw pictures of it.

What happened first?

What happened next?

What happened last?

With the help of an adult, write what is happening in your drawings.

Storytelling

Upon completion, add these stickers to your path on the map!

BONUS: What do you hope you'll do next summer?

Now add this sticker to your map!

Community

Friendly Town

Look at the picture of downtown. Follow the directions to color the picture.

Upon completion, add this sticker to your path on the map!

The mayor works at City Hall. Color City Hall **purple**.

Judges work at the courthouse. Color the courthouse **green**.

People live in apartments. They grow flowers in their window boxes. Color the apartment building **blue**.

Storytime

Look at the story. Circle the characters. Then color the setting of the story.

Storytelling

Upon completion, add this sticker to your path on the map!

Brain Box

Characters do the actions in the story.

The **setting** is where the story takes place.

Seasons

Draw a line to match the picture with the season.

Upon completion, add these stickers to your path on the map!

Summer

Fall

Winter

Spring

| Summer | Fall | Winter | Spring |

Seasons

BONUS: Circle the picture of the tornado.

Now add this sticker to your map!

Patterns

What Comes Next?

Look at the windows on the doors. Do you see a pattern? Use the pattern to draw the next shape.

Look at the pattern. Draw the next item in the pattern.

Look at the row of pool towels. Use the pattern to color the next pool towels.

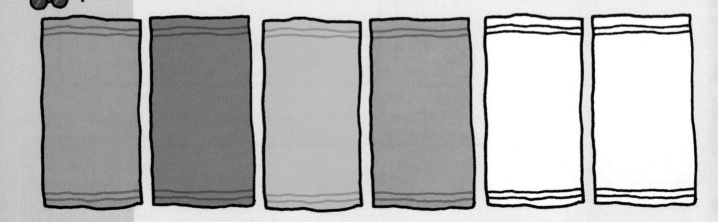

Look at the fish in the creek. Use the pattern to color the next fish.

Look at the caterpillars and butterflies. Use the pattern to color the next 2.

BONUS: Draw six beach balls. Color them to make a pattern.

Upon completion, add these stickers to your path on the map!

Now add this sticker to your map!

Counting

Beach Day

You're going to the beach! Circle the things you might wear or bring to the beach. Then count how many items you have circled.

Upon completion, add this sticker to your path on the map!

BONUS: How many things did you circle?

_____

Now add this sticker to your map!

Level 5 complete!

Add this achievement sticker
to your path...

...and move on to

Level 6!

Reading

Book Cover

Look at the cover of the big yellow book. Circle the title. Underline the names of the author and the illustrator.

NOP QRSTU VW XYZ

SHAPES PROJECT

BOOK WEEK!

BOOKS   WEATHER   BALLS   BOOKS

WORMS!

BLOCKS   BLOCKS   SHAPES

KANGAROO'S FIRST DAY OF SCHOOL

Words by Willa Bee
Pictures by Mac Rufus

Brain Box

A **title** is the name of a book.

The **author** writes the words.

The **illustrator** draws the pictures.

Our Flag

Follow the directions to color the American flag.

My Country

The stars are white. Color the space around them **blue**.

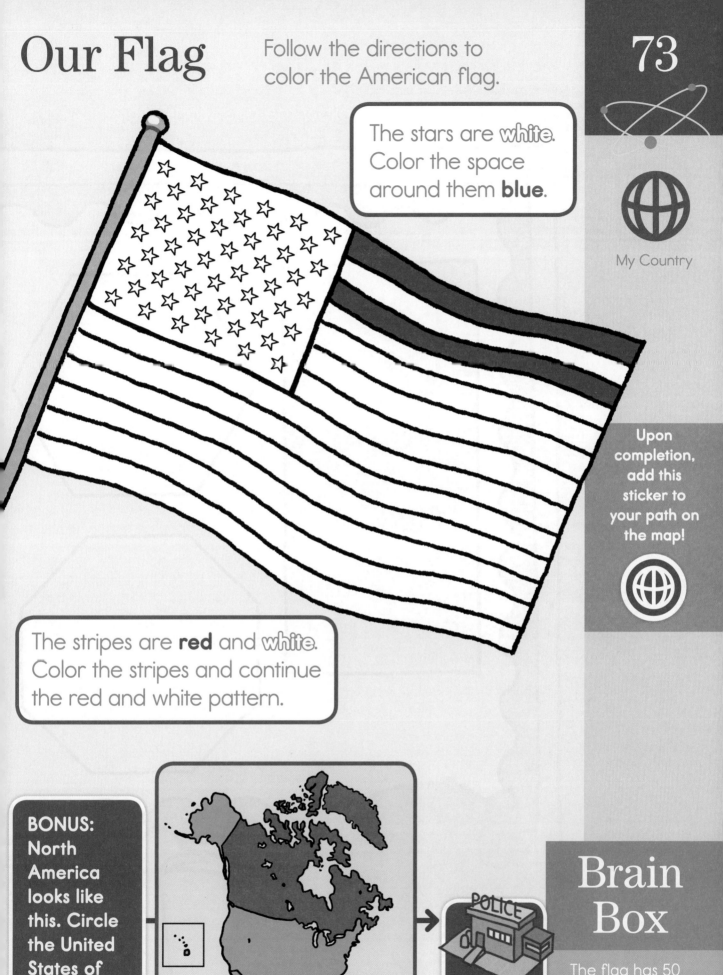

Upon completion, add this sticker to your path on the map!

The stripes are **red** and white. Color the stripes and continue the red and white pattern.

BONUS: North America looks like this. Circle the United States of America on the map.

POLICE

Now add this sticker to your map!

Brain Box

The flag has 50 white stars for the 50 US states.

The flag has 13 stripes for the first 13 US colonies.

Shape Challenge

Look at the shapes. Follow the directions.

Shapes

Brain Box

A **square** has four sides.
A **pentagon** has five sides.
A **hexagon** has six sides.
An **octagon** has eight sides.

Color the square **blue**.
Color the hexagon **green**.
Color the octagon **red**.

Shapes

PIZZA PARTY
MONDAY

Upon
completion,
add these
stickers to
your path on
the map!

BONUS: Can you
draw a shape that
has more sides than
a square, but fewer
sides than a hexagon?
Color it purple.

Now add this
sticker
to your
map!

Landforms

Look at the picture. Say the names of the landforms. Color the bodies of water **blue**. Color the land **green**.

Upon completion, add these stickers to your path on the map!

hills

plains

Brain Box

Landforms are parts of the shape of the land. They include mountains, hills, plains, valleys, and islands.

Landforms

mountains

river

island

pond

BONUS: Pick a landform. Name an animal that might live there.

Now add this sticker to your map!

Sentences

We Love Books!

Read the sentences. Circle the first word.
Draw a line under the second word.
Color over the last word with yellow.

Upon completion, add this sticker to your path on the map!

I like books.

She reads fast.

He reads quietly.

We are readers.

Big Numbers

10 students are at the drinking fountain. More join them!
Trace the number of total students.

123s

$10 + 1 =$ 11

$10 + 2 =$ 12

$10 + 3 =$ 13

$10 + 4 =$ 14

$10 + 5 =$ 15

Upon completion, add this sticker to your path on the map!

BONUS: There are 10 buses. Draw 1 more. Count the buses. How many are there?

Now add this sticker to your map!

Old School

Look at the two classrooms. The classroom on the left is 100 years old. The classroom on the right is new.

One hundred years ago, teachers taught all different ages at the same time. Today's teacher is teaching kindergartners. Circle both teachers.

Today's students use pencil and paper or computers for writing. Students 100 years ago wrote on slates with chalk. Circle the students who are using chalk.

Today's students sometimes arrive in buses. Students 100 years ago walked to school. Color the buses yellow.

Past and Present

BONUS: Color the rest of both pictures however you like.

Now add this sticker to your map!

Syllables

Look at the syllables of each word. Write them as one word to make the word shown in the picture.

mit	ten

mitten

kit	ten

ro	bot

lad	der

Brain Box

A word has one or more **syllables**. Syllables are beats in the word. You could clap for each syllable.
Row (clap) has one syllable. **Robot** (clap, clap) has two.

Who Am I?

Trace the words. Fill in the blanks with your name and age. Then circle the things you like.

My name is

_____ .

I am _____ years old.

I like

Read the sentences above aloud. Say the words for the things you like.

BONUS: Complete the sentence using the right word, I or My.

_____ love school.

Now add this sticker to your map!

Shapes

Compare and Contrast

Look at the shapes. Count the corners. Write the number of corners for each shape.

Circle the two shapes that have the same number of corners.

Look at the sides of each shape.
Color the shape if all its sides
are the same size.

Shapes

Upon
completion,
add these
stickers to
your path on
the map!

You Are, She Is

You and your sister are opposites.
Trace or write **You** or **She**, and **are** or **is**.

Spelling and
Vocabulary

Upon completion, add this sticker to your path on the map!

You are tall.

She is short.

You are awake.

She is asleep.

You are loud.

WAAH

Now she is loud, too.

Level 6 complete!

Add this achievement sticker
to your path…

…and move on to

Level 7!

Letter Detective

Look at each set of words. The words have some letters that are the same. The words also have some letters that are different. Underline the letters that are **different**.

slide  ride

boat  float

Look at each set of words. Underline the letters that are the **same**.

bat  hat

swing  ring

Fun Then and Now

Look at the toys children played with 200 years ago. Look at the toys children play with today.

Say how each pair is different. Which toy would you rather play with, the old one or new one?

Past and Present

Upon completion, add this sticker to your path on the map!

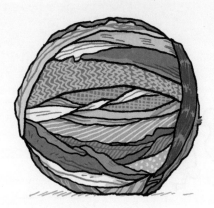

Addition

Upon completion, add this sticker to your path on the map!

Petting Zoo

Count the animals in both pictures. Then write the total number.

+ =

+ =

+ =

QUACK

+ =

Race!

The friends are racing their toy cars down the slide. Look at each picture. Circle which car you think will win. Say why.

Motion

Upon completion, add this sticker to your path on the map!

The Three Little Pigs

Look at the illustrations. Tell the story of the Three Little Pigs.

Reading

Reading

Upon completion, add these stickers to your path on the map!

Shapes

Flat or Solid?

Circle the flat shapes. Draw an **X** through the solid shapes.

Upon completion, add this sticker to your path on the map!

Brain Box

2-D shapes are flat, like this:

3-D shapes are solid and have volume, like this:

There's a Shape for That

Look at the 3-D shapes. Match each 3-D shape to the object that has the same shape.

Upon completion, add this sticker to your path on the map!

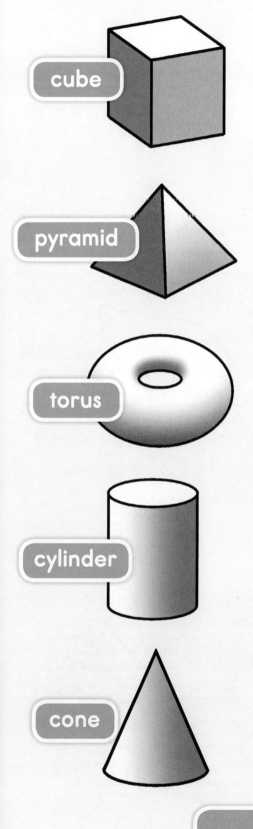

cube

pyramid

torus

cylinder

cone

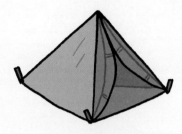

BONUS: Color the sphere so that it looks like your favorite type of ball.

Now add this sticker to your map!

Living Things

People and animals change the world around them in many ways. What happens first, second, third, and fourth? Write numbers to put them in order.

What happens first, second, third, and fourth?
Write numbers to put them in order.

Living Things

Upon completion, add these stickers to your path on the map!

Merry-Go-Round

Sentences begin with an uppercase letter.
Trace the first letter in each sentence.

Uppercase
Letters

Upon
completion,
add this
sticker to
your path on
the map!

Let's get in line.

It costs $3.

$3 PER RIDE

I like the blue horse.

This is fun!

Problem at the Park

Read about the problem. Then say aloud what the kids should do.

There are two bouncy balls.

But there is only one field.

We want to play kickball.

We want to play soccer.

What should we do?

Community

Draw a picture that shows a fair solution.

Upon completion, add this sticker to your path on the map!

BONUS: Draw a picture of two animals sharing a toy.

Now add this sticker to your map!

Time

Morning and Night

Circle all the things you do in the morning.

Circle all the things you do at night.

Upon completion, add these stickers to your path on the map!

Now add this sticker to your map!

BONUS: Draw a picture of your favorite thing to do in the afternoon.

Zoo Babies

Most sentences end with a period (.). Add a period at the end of each sentence.

Writing

The cubs play.

The kittens snuggle

The baby climbs

Upon completion, add this sticker to your path on the map!

The kids jump

Mixed-Up Colors

The colors are mixed up! Complete the sentences about the painting.

Writing

green

blue

pink

The sky is

The grass is

The pig is

Upon completion, add this sticker to your path on the map!

BONUS: Draw your own picture with mixed-up colors.

Now add this sticker to your map!

Shapes in a Row

Look at the shapes. Do you see a pattern?
Use the pattern to draw the next shape.

Patterns

Upon completion, add this sticker to your path on the map!

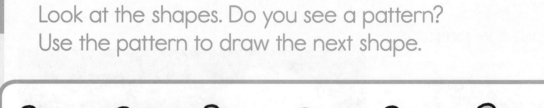

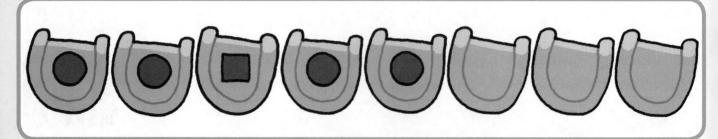

Level 7
complete!

Add this achievement sticker
to your path…

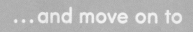

…and move on to

Level
8!

Read the sentences.
Trace the question mark (**?**)
or exclamation point (**!**).

Writing

Upon completion, add this sticker to your path on the map!

Here comes the airplane!

Is Nana on the plane?

Let's go see!

Brain Box

A question mark (**?**) ends a sentence that is a question. An exclamation point (**!**) ends a sentence that is a shout, or an exclamation.

She and Papa are both here. Yay!

Days of the Week

The train has a dining car. The calendar shows what is for lunch each day.

Circle the lunch you would like to eat the most.

Calendar

Sunday	
Monday	
Tuesday	
Wednesday	
Thursday	
Friday	
Saturday	

Upon completion, add this sticker to your path on the map!

BONUS: Write the day of the week that this lunch is served.

Now add this sticker to your map!

Properties

Sink or Float?

Fill a bowl with water.
Get two small objects
that are OK to put in water.
Do you think the items will float or sink?

Place the first object in the water. Draw a picture
of what happened. Did it float or sink?

Upon
completion,
add this
sticker to
your path on
the map!

Place the second object in the water. Draw a picture
of what happened. Did it float or sink?

Going Places

Look at the map.

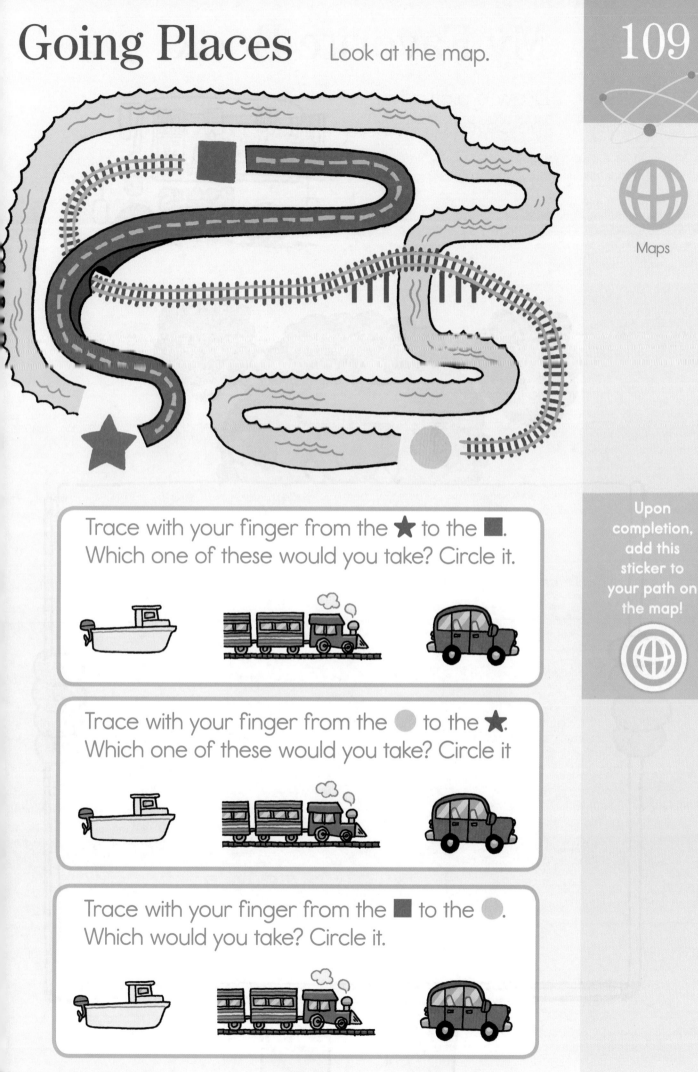

Trace with your finger from the ★ to the ■.
Which one of these would you take? Circle it.

Trace with your finger from the ● to the ★.
Which one of these would you take? Circle it

Trace with your finger from the ■ to the ●.
Which would you take? Circle it.

Upon completion, add this sticker to your path on the map!

My Favorite Book

Draw a picture of the cover of your favorite book.

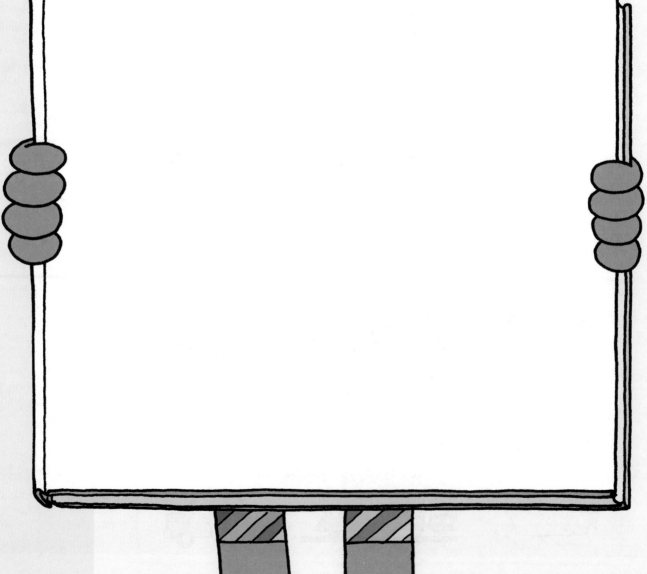

Write a sentence about why you like this book.
(Ask for help writing if you need it.)

Writing

Upon completion, add these stickers to your path on the map!

BONUS: What book would you write? Draw the cover here.

Now add this sticker to your map!

Calendar

12 Terrific Months

There are 12 months in the year. Point to each one in order. Look at the picture of what is special about that month.

January

HAPPY NEW YEAR'S DAY!

February

March

April

May

June

Circle your favorite month. Write that month:

Draw an **X** next to your birthday month.
Write that month.

July

August

September

October

November

December

Draw a book next to the month you start school.
Write that month.

Upon completion, add these stickers to your path on the map!

BONUS:
What is the first month of the year?

Now add this sticker to your map!

Reading Signs

Each sign has one or two words. Point to each sign. What does it say?

Reading

Upon completion, add this sticker to your path on the map!

Trucks, Buses, and Trains

Compare each object.

Circle the **longer** train.

Upon completion, add this sticker to your path on the map!

Circle the **taller** bus.

Circle the **heavier** dump truck.

States

My Home State

Learn about your state symbols. Ask an adult to help you find the information in a book or online.

Color in your state.

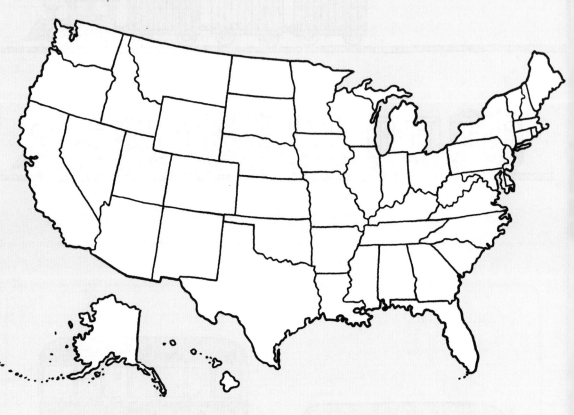

Upon completion, add this sticker to your path on the map!

Draw a picture of your state bird.

Draw a picture of your state flower.

Duck. Duck!

One word can mean different things. Draw a line to match the pictures that share the same word.

Spelling and Vocabulary

Upon completion, add this sticker to your path on the map!

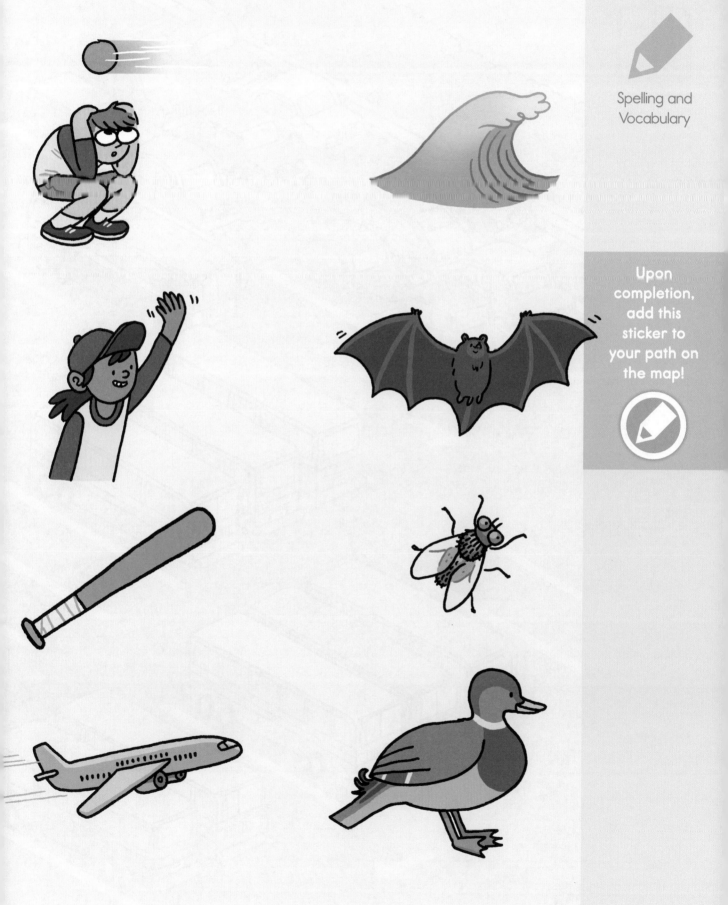

123s

Travel Time!

The cars and buses are parked at the airport.

Upon completion, add these stickers to your path on the map!

Count as many cars and buses as you can aloud!

AIRPORT

123s

BONUS: Write the number of cars and buses you counted.

_____

cars and buses

Now add this sticker to your map!

Water Changes

Look at the ways water can change.

Water

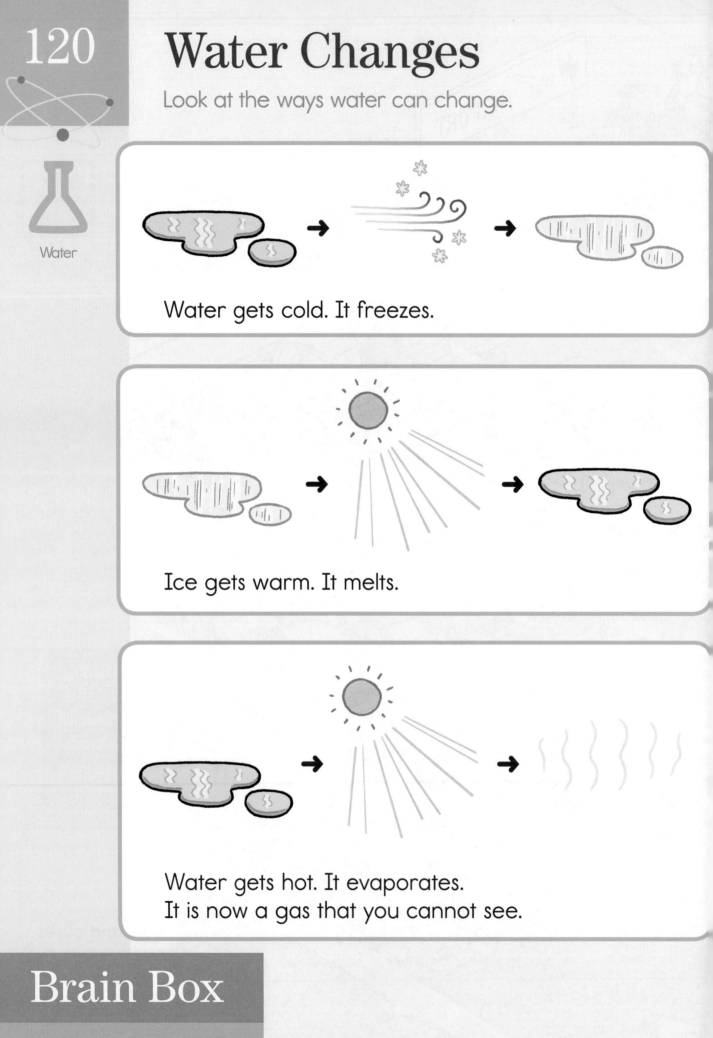

Water gets cold. It freezes.

Ice gets warm. It melts.

Water gets hot. It evaporates.
It is now a gas that you cannot see.

Brain Box

Water can change by **freezing**, **melting**, or **evaporating**.

Look at each pair of scenes. They show water changing. But one pair is wrong. Draw an **X** through the one that is wrong.

Water

Upon completion, add these stickers to your path on the map!

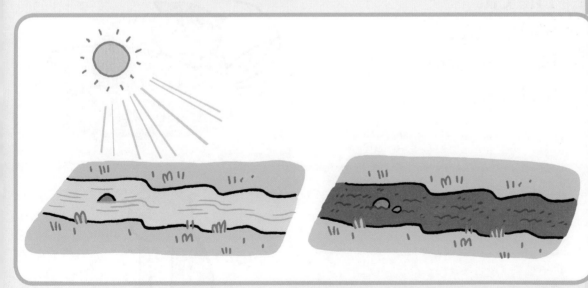

CONGRATULATIONS!
You completed all of your science quests! You earned:

The Cat Is Sick

Read the sentences. Draw a line to match each sentence with its picture.

Upon completion, add this sticker to your path on the map!

The cat is sick.

He goes to bed.

The cat wakes up. How do you feel, cat?

He feels better now.

More or Less?

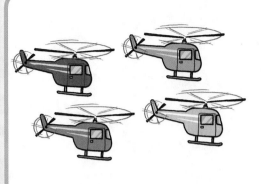 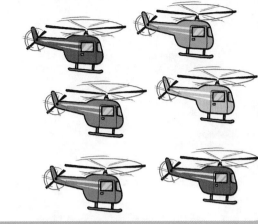

Comparing

Upon completion, add this sticker to your path on the map!

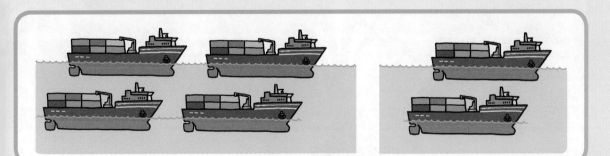

CONGRATULATIONS!
You completed all of your math quests! You earned:

Countries

The Fourth of July

Color the fireworks **red**, **white**, and **blue**.

Brain Box

The **Fourth of July** is when America declared its independence. It's a day we celebrate every year!

Countries

Upon completion, add these stickers to your path on the map!

CONGRATULATIONS! You completed all of your social studies quests! You earned:

ABC You Later!

Uh-oh! Some of the letters in the alphabet have disappeared. Can you trace the dotted letters and write the missing ones?

ABCs

Upon completion, add this sticker to your path on the map!

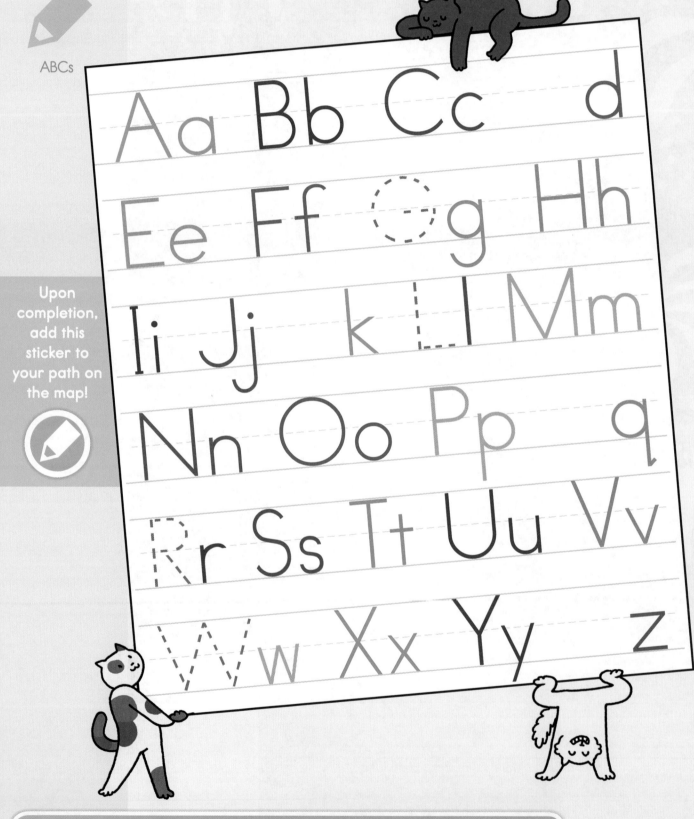

Aa Bb Cc d
Ee Ff g Hh
Ii Jj k L Mm
Nn Oo Pp q
R Ss Tt Uu Vv
W w Xx Yy z

Quest
complete!

Add this achievement sticker to your path…

QUEST complete! Welcome to kindergarten!

…and turn to the next page for your Summer Brainiac Award!

Summer Brainiac Award!

You have completed your entire Summer Brain Quest! Woo-hoo! Congratulations! That's quite an achievement.

Write your name on the line and cut out the award certificate. Show your friends. Hang it on your wall! You're a certified Summer Brainiac!

Summer Brainiac Award

Presented to:

_____

for successfully completing the learning journey in

SUMMER BRAIN QUEST®: BETWEEN GRADES PRE-K & K

Outside Quests

This is not just a workbook—it's an exotic expedition, a flight through foreign lands, a way to enjoy the summer sunshine, and so much more! Summer is the perfect time to explore the great outdoors. Use the Outside Quests to make your next sunny day more fun than ever—and earn an achievement sticker.

Level 1 Bug Detective

In your yard or on a playground, find a small animal, such as a snail, ant, or ladybug. Observe it for as long as you can. Draw a picture of it and the things around it. Circle anything it was eating or carrying. Use an arrow to show where it was going.

Now add this sticker to your map!

Level 2 Water Work

Do a water experiment. Fill two containers with one cup of water each. Cover one container. Leave the other uncovered. Place both containers in the sun. Every morning for one week, measure how much water is left in each container. Draw a picture to show what happened.

Now add this sticker to your map!

Level 2 — Nature Game

Use natural resources found in your yard or playground (such as sticks and stones) to make a game, like tic-tac-toe or something new. Describe the goal of the game and the rules. Play the game with someone.

Now add this sticker to your map!

Level 3 — Celebrate!

Prepare a special picnic food to celebrate an important day for your family, community, or country. (It could also be a silly day like National Popcorn Day.) Be sure to help clean up.

Now add this sticker to your map!

Now add
this sticker
to your
map!

Level 5 — Speedways

Find two balls that are the same size. Using blocks, boards, or books, make two ramps the same length. One should be steeper than the other. Race the balls down the ramp. Which finishes faster?

Level 6 — ABC Hop

Write the alphabet using sidewalk chalk, then sing the alphabet song while hopping on each letter!

Now add
this sticker
to your
map!

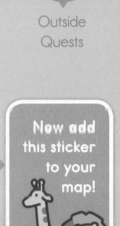

Outside
Quests

Level 7 ▸ Bugs vs Birds

Go on a counting walk in your yard or a nearby park. Write a tally of how many bugs you see. Keep a tally of how many birds you see. Did you see more bugs or birds?

Now add this sticker to your map!

Level 8 ▸ Stick Letters

Gather fallen sticks or stems. Use them to make letters. Count how many sticks it takes to make each letter.

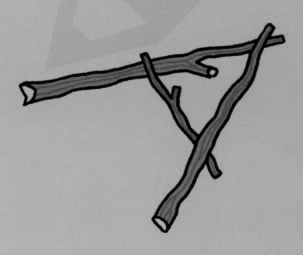

Now add this sticker to your map!

Answer Key

(For pages or answers not included
in this section, answers will vary.)

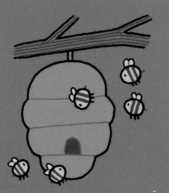

Your Name

10 Circle the first letter of your first name in uppercase. Then underline the lowercase letters that are in your first name.

Aa Bb Cc Dd
Ee Ff Gg Hh
Ii Jj Kk Ll Mm
Nn Oo Pp Qq
Rr Ss Tt Uu Vv
Ww Xx Yy Zz

Now write your name.

Answers will vary.

Count

11 Count the items in each set. Then trace the number.

1 firetruck
2 firefighters
3 trees
4 cats
5 children

My Family

12 Look at each activity. Circle one activity you like to do with your family.

Draw a picture of your family doing your favorite activity.

Answers will vary.

The Five Senses

13 Draw a line from the picture to the sense that goes best with it.

hear
see
smell
touch
taste

Brain Box

ABCDEF

14 Trace the uppercase and lowercase letters. Then write the uppercase and lowercase letters. Say the name of the object that begins with that letter.

A A A A A
a a a a a
B B B B B
b b b b b
C C C C C
c c c c c

15
D D D D D
d d d d d
L L L L L
e e e e e
F F F F F
f f f f f

BONUS: Draw something that starts with the letter b.

Answers will vary.

Cat-astrophe!

16 Look at the neighborhood. Follow the directions to color the picture.

17 Color the firetruck **red**.
Color the cat **orange**.
Color the bird **blue**.
Color the dog walker's shirt **purple**.
Color the tree trunk **brown**.
Color the leaves and grass **green**.
Color the house **yellow**.

BONUS: What color comes from mixing red and blue? Color the doghouse that color.

purple

GHI

18 Trace the uppercase and lowercase letters. Then write the uppercase and lowercase letters. Say the name of the object that begins with that letter.

G G G G G
g g g g g
H H H H H
h h h h h
I I I I I
i i i i i

JKL

20 Trace the uppercase and lowercase letters. Then write the uppercase and lowercase letters. Say the name of the object that begins with that letter.

J J J J J
j j j j j
K K K K K
k k k k k
L L L L L

Farm to Market

21 Read about the workers. Then follow the directions.

The **farmer** grows the wheat.
Draw a line under the farmer.
The **miller** grinds the wheat into flour.
Draw a circle around the miller.
The **baker** uses the flour to bake bread.
Draw a triangle around the baker.
The **grocer** sells the bread at her store.
Draw a square around the grocer.

Watermelon Patch

22 Animals are playing in the watermelon patch!

23 Count the number of each type of animal in the watermelon patch. Find the box with the name of that animal. Then trace the number.

6 squirrels
7 birds
8 mice
9 toads
10 bees

BONUS: How many flies are there? Write the number.

11 flies

MNO

24 Trace the uppercase and lowercase letters. Then write the uppercase and lowercase letters. Say the name of the object that begins with that letter.

M M M M M
m m m m m
N N N N N
n n n n n
O O O O O
o o o o o

Lunch Time!

25 Look at the map of the farm. Start at the pond and draw a line along the path to the farmhouse.

BONUS: Bees make honey and live in beehives. Find the beehive on the map and circle it.

PQRST

Trace the uppercase and lowercase letters. Then write the uppercase and lowercase letters. Say the name of the object that begins with that letter.

Letters: PQRST

Upon completion, add these stickers to your path on the map!

P P P P P
p p p p p

Q Q Q Q Q
q q q q q

R R R R R
r r r r r

S S S S S
s s s s s

T T T T T
t t t t t

Letters: PQRST

BONUS: What letter are the chicks forming?

S

Now add this sticker to your map!

Fun Shapes

Shapes

Trace the circle. Then draw your own circle. Color your circle **orange**, like an orange.

Upon completion, add these stickers to your path on the map!

Trace the triangle. Then draw your own triangle. Color your triangle **yellow**, like a slice of cheese.

Trace the rectangle. Then draw your own rectangle. Make your rectangle into a garden by coloring it **green**.

Shapes

Trace the square. Then draw your own square. Make your square into a pool by coloring it **blue**.

My Plant and Me

Habitats

Draw a line from the child to the things she needs. Draw a line from the plant to the things it needs. (**Hint:** There are two things that both plants and people need.)

Upon completion, add this sticker to your path on the map!

Brain Box

People and plants are living things. But a person and plant need different things to grow.

Safety Rules

Community

Look at the picture. Color the things that keep people safe.

Color the hard hats **yellow**. They protect the workers' heads.
Color the goggles **gray**. They protect the workers' eyes.
Color the gloves **red**. They protect the workers' hands.
Color the cones **orange**. They keep other people out of the construction zone.

Tool Time

Look at the pictures. Circle the tool that would help with the job.

Tools

Upon completion, add this sticker to your path on the map!

UVWXYZ

Trace the uppercase and lowercase letters. Then write the uppercase and lowercase letters. Say the name of the object that begins with that letter.

Letters: UVWXYZ

U U U U U
u u u u u

V V V V V
v v v v v

W W W W W
w w w w w

Trace and write the letters. Say the name of the object that **ends** with the letter.

X X X X X
x x x x x

Trace and write the letters. Say the name of the object that **begins** with that letter.

Y Y Y Y Y
y y y y y

Z Z Z Z Z
z z z z z

Letters: UVWXYZ

Upon completion, add these stickers to your path on the map!

WALK

Two Shapes Together

Shapes

Trace the line to make the square into two triangles.

Trace the two lines to make the triangle into a square.

Draw two touching squares to make a rectangle.

Upon completion, add this sticker to your path on the map!

Home Sweet Home

Draw a line from the animal to its habitat.

Habitats

Alligators eat animals, but deer eat plants. Circle some of the things the deer might eat.

Brain Box

Unlock two different habitats. The harder key for and shelter for the animals.

AEIOU

Say the word that describes the picture aloud. Then circle the letter that completes the word. Write the missing letter to complete the word.

Vowels

dig o i

cup a u

hat a o

Answers will vary.

Vowels

Upon completion, add these stickers to your path on the map!

ten e o

10

BONUS: What words can you write? Write a word on the construction worker's sign.

Now add this sticker to your map!

Shapes Are Everywhere!

Shapes

Look at the picture. Then follow the directions.

PIZZA

STOP

GROCERY

Answers will vary.

Shapes

Upon completion, add these stickers to your path on the map!

BONUS: The excavator will pick up oval-shaped stones. It will not pick up circle-shaped stones. Color the stones that the excavator will pick up purple.

Now add this sticker to your map!

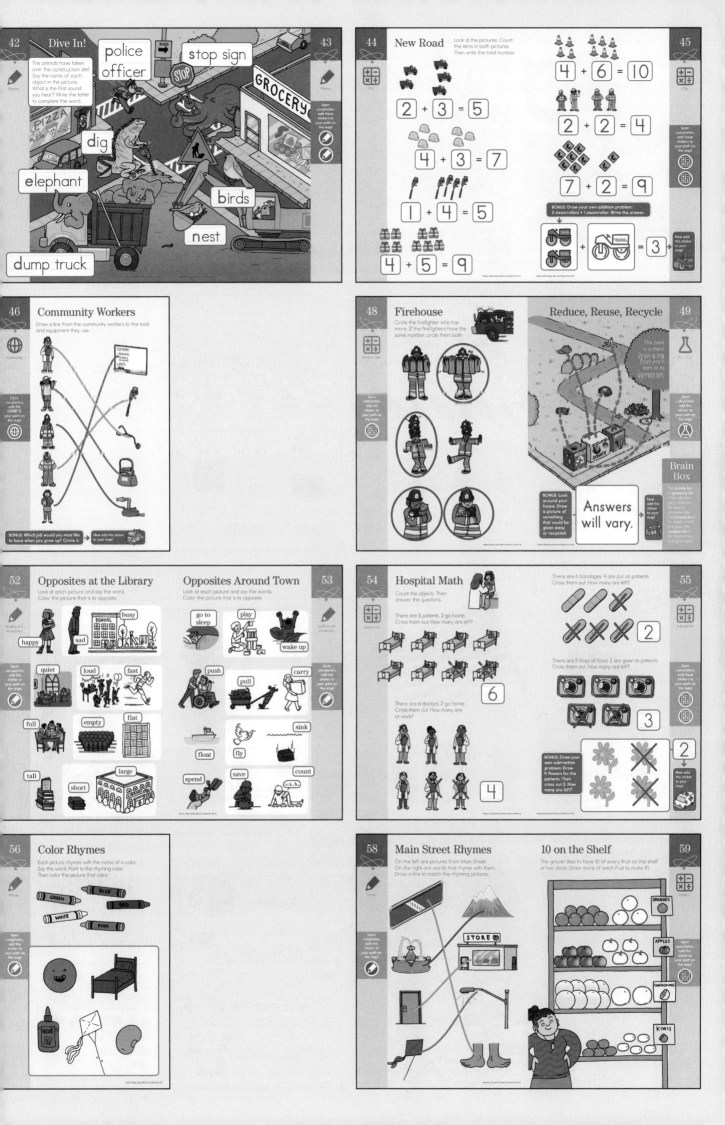

42 — Dive In!

The animals have taken over the construction site! Say the name of each object in the picture. What is the first sound you hear? Write the letter to complete the word.

police officer
stop sign
GROCERY
PIZZA
dig
elephant
birds
nest
dump truck

43

44 — New Road

Look at the pictures. Count the items in both pictures. Then write the total number.

2 + 3 = 5

4 + 6 = 10

2 + 2 = 4

4 + 3 = 7

7 + 2 = 9

1 + 4 = 5

4 + 5 = 9

BONUS: Draw your own addition problem: 2 steamrollers + 1 steamroller. Write the answer.

+ = 3

45

46 — Community Workers

Draw a line from the community workers to the tools and equipment they use.

BONUS: Which job would you most like to have when you grow up? Circle it.

48 — Firehouse

Circle the firefighter who has more. If the firefighters have the same number, circle them both.

BONUS: Look around your house. Draw a picture of something that could be given away or recycled.

49 — Reduce, Reuse, Recycle

This park is a mess! Draw a line from each item to its correct bin.

Brain Box

Answers will vary.

52 — Opposites at the Library

Look at each picture and say the word. Color the picture that is its opposite.

happy — sad — busy
quiet — loud — fast
full — empty — flat
tall — short — large

53 — Opposites Around Town

Look at each picture and say the words. Color the picture that is its opposite.

go to sleep — play — wake up
push — pull — carry
float — fly — sink
spend — save — count

54 — Hospital Math

Count the objects. Then answer the questions.

There are 8 patients. 2 go home. Cross them out. How many are left?

6

There are 6 doctors. 2 go home. Cross them out. How many are at work?

4

There are 6 bandages. 4 are put on patients. Cross them out. How many are left?

2

There are 5 trays of food. 2 are given to patients. Cross them out. How many are left?

3

BONUS: Draw your own subtraction problem: Draw 4 flowers for the patients. Then cross out 2. How many are left?

2

55

56 — Color Rhymes

Each picture rhymes with the name of a color. Say the word. Point to the rhyming color. Then color the picture that color.

GREEN BLUE RED
WHITE PINK
GLUE

58 — Main Street Rhymes

On the left are pictures from Main Street. On the right are words that rhyme with them. Draw a line to match the rhyming pictures.

STORE

59 — 10 on the Shelf

The grocer likes to have 10 of every fruit on the shelf at her store. Draw more of each fruit to make 10.

ORANGES
APPLES
CANTALOUPES
KIWIS

64

Friendly Town

Look at the picture of downtown. Follow the directions to color the picture.

The mayor works at City Hall. Color City Hall **purple**.
Judges work at the courthouse. Color the courthouse **green**.
People live in apartments. They grow flowers in their window boxes.
Color the apartment building **blue**.

Storytime

Look at the story. Circle the characters. Then color the setting of the story.

Brain Box

Characters are the people in the story.
The **setting** is where the story takes place.

Seasons

Draw a line to match the picture with the season.

Summer
Fall
Winter
Spring

Write the name of the right season below each picture.

| Summer | Fall | Winter | Spring |

Winter   Spring
Summer   Fall

BONUS: Circle the picture of the tornado.

Now add this sticker to your map!

What Comes Next?

Look at the windows on the doors. Do you see a pattern? Use the pattern to draw the next shape.

Look at the pattern. Draw the next item in the pattern.

Look at the row of pool towels. Use the pattern to color the next pool towels.

Look at the fish in the creek. Use the pattern to color the next fish.

Look at the caterpillars and butterflies. Use the pattern to color the next 2.

BONUS: Draw six beach balls. Color them to make a pattern.

Answers will vary.

Now add this sticker to your map!

Beach Day

You're going to the beach! Circle the things you might wear or bring to the beach. Then count how many items you have circled.

BONUS: How many things did you circle? **8**

Now add this sticker to your map!

Book Cover

Look at the cover of the big yellow book. Circle the title. Underline the names of the author and the illustrator.

KANGAROO'S FIRST DAY OF SCHOOL

Words by Willa Bee
Pictures by Mac Rufus

Brain Box

A **title** is the name of a book. The **author** writes the words. The **illustrator** draws the pictures.

Our Flag

Follow the directions to color the American flag.

The stars are **white**. Color the space around them **blue**.

The stripes are **red** and **white**. Color the stripes and continue the red and white pattern.

BONUS: North America looks like this. Circle the United States of America on the map.

Brain Box

The flag has 50 white stars for the 50 US states.

The flag has 13 stripes for the 13 original US colonies.

Now add this sticker to your map!

Shape Challenge

Look at the shapes. Follow the directions.

LEARN TO SWIM!
MONDAY
WEDNESDAY
FRIDAY
2 - 3 PM
AT THE POOL

PIZZA PARTY MONDAY

Color the square **blue**.
Color the hexagon **green**.
Color the octagon **red**.

BONUS: Can you draw a shape that has more sides than a square, but fewer sides than a hexagon? Color it **green**.

Brain Box

A **square** has four sides. A **pentagon** has five sides. A **hexagon** has six sides. An **octagon** has eight sides.

Now add this sticker to your map!

Landforms

Look at the picture. Say the names of the landforms. Color the bodies of water **blue**. Color the land **green**.

hills
plains
mountains
river
island
pond

Brain Box

Landforms are parts of the shape of the land. They include mountains, hills, plains, valleys, and islands.

BONUS: Pick a landform. Name an animal that might live there.

Now add this sticker to your map!

We Love Books!

Read the sentences. Circle the first word. Draw a line under the second word. Color over the last word with **yellow**.

I like books.
She reads fast.
He reads quietly.
We are readers.

Big Numbers

10 students are at the drinking fountain. More join them! Trace the number of total students.

79

$$10 + 1 = 11$$
$$10 + 2 = 12$$
$$10 + 3 = 13$$
$$10 + 4 = 14$$
$$10 + 5 = 15$$

BONUS: There are 10 buses. Draw 1 more. Count the buses. How many are there? **11**

Now add this sticker to your map!

Old School

Look at the two classrooms. The classroom on the left is 100 years old. The classroom on the right is new.

One hundred years ago, teachers taught all different ages at the same time. Today's teacher is teaching kindergartners. Circle both teachers.

Today's students use pencil and paper or computers for writing. Students 100 years ago wrote on slates with chalk. Circle the students who are using chalk.

Today's students sometimes arrive in buses. Students 100 years ago walked to school. Color the buses yellow.

BONUS: Circle the rest of both pictures however you like.

Now add this sticker to your map!

Syllables

Look at the syllables of each word. Write them as one word to make the word shown in the picture.

mit | ten
mitten

kit | ten
kitten

ro | bot
robot

lad | der
ladder

Brain Box

A word has one or more **syllables**. Syllables are breaks in the word. You can tap, clap, for each syllable.
Row (clap) has one syllable. **Robot** (clap-clap) has two.

Who Am I?

Trace the words. Fill in the blanks with your name and age. Then circle the things you like.

My name is _____.

I am ____ years old.

I like

Read the sentences above aloud. Say the words for the things you like.

BONUS: Complete the sentence using the right word, I or My.

___ love school.

Now add this sticker to your map!

Compare and Contrast

Look at the shapes. Count the corners. Write the number of corners for each shape.

Circle the two shapes that have the same number of corners.

4

3

5

4

Look at the sides of each shape. Color the shape if all its sides are the same size.

Now add this sticker to your map!

You Are, She Is

You and your sister are opposites. Trace or write You or She, and are or is.

You are tall.

She is short.

You are awake.

She is asleep.

You are loud.

Now she is loud, too.

Letter Detective

Look at each set of words. The words have some letters that are the same. The words also have some letters that are different. Underline the letters that are different.

s̲lide · r̲ide

b̲oat · fl̲oat

Look at each set of words. Underline the letters that are the same.

bat · hat

swing · ring

Fun Then and Now

Look at the toys children played with 200 years ago. Look at the toys children play with today.

Say how each pair is different. Which toy would you rather play with, the old one or new one?

Possible Answers: The action figure comes in a box and is more colorful. The toys are made of different materials.

The cornhusk doll is more plain, and the new doll is more colorful. The cornhusk doll is homemade, and the new doll is from a store.

The rag ball is homemade, and the new ball comes from a store.

Now add this sticker to your path on the map!

Petting Zoo

Count the animals in both pictures. Then write the total number.

☐ + ☐ = 7

☐ + ☐ = 4

☐ + ☐ = 9

☐ + ☐ = 8

Race!

The friends are racing their toy cars down the slide. Look at each picture. Circle which car you think will win. Say why.

Possible Answer: The bumps will slow down the car on the bumpy path, but the car on the smooth path has no bumps to slow it down.

Flat or Solid?

Circle the flat shapes. Draw an X through the solid shapes.

Brain Box

There's a Shape for That

Look at the 3-D shapes. Match each 3-D shape to the object that has the same shape.

cube

pyramid

torus

cylinder

cone

BONUS: Color the sphere so that it looks like your favorite type of ball.

Answers will vary.

Now add this sticker to your map!

Living Things

People and animals change the world around them in many ways. What happens first, second, third, and fourth? Write numbers to put them in order.

3

2

1

4

What happens first, second, third, and fourth? Write numbers to put them in order.

1

3

2

4

Merry-Go-Round

Sentences begin with an uppercase letter. Trace the first letter in each sentence.

Uppercase Letters

Let's get in line.

It costs $3.

$3 PER RIDE

I like the blue horse.

This is fun!

Problem at the Park

Read about the problem. Then say aloud what the kids should do.

There are two bouncy balls.
But there is only one field.
We want to play soccer.
We want to play kickball.
What should we do?

Draw a picture that shows a fair solution.

One possible solution: Divide the field in two, with one side for soccer and the other for kickball. Another solution: Take turns playing soccer and kickball on the field.

BONUS: Draw a picture of two animals sharing a toy.

Now add this sticker to your map!

Community

Morning and Night

Circle all the things you do in the morning.

Time

Circle all the things you do at night.

Time

BONUS: Draw a picture of your favorite thing to do in the afternoon.

Now add this sticker to your map!

Zoo Babies

Most sentences end with a period (.). Add a period at the end of each sentence.

Writing

The cubs play.

The kittens snuggle.

The baby climbs.

The kids jump.

Mixed-Up Colors

The colors are mixed up! Complete the sentences about the painting.

green
blue
pink

The sky is **green**.
The grass is **pink**.
The pig is **blue**.

Writing

BONUS: Draw your own picture with mixed-up colors.

Now add this sticker to your map!

Shapes in a Row

Look at the shapes. Do you see a pattern? Use the pattern to draw the next shape.

Patterns

Airport

Read the sentences. Trace the question mark (?) or exclamation point (!).

Writing

Here comes the airplane!

Is Nana on the plane?

Let's go see!

Brain Box
A question mark (?) ends a sentence that is a question. An exclamation point (!) ends a sentence that is about or an exclamation.

She and Papa are both here. Yay!

Days of the Week

The train has a dining car. The calendar shows what is for lunch each day. Circle the lunch you would like to eat the most.

Sunday	
Monday	
Tuesday	
Wednesday	
Thursday	
Friday	
Saturday	

Calendar

BONUS: Write the day of the week that this lunch is served.

Answers will vary.

Now add this sticker to your map!

Going Places Look at the map.

Maps

Trace with your finger from the ★ to the ■. Which one of these would you take? Circle it.

Trace with your finger from the ● to the ★. Which one of these would you take? Circle it.

Trace with your finger from the ■ to the ●. Which would you take? Circle it.

---

12 Terrific Months

There are 12 months in the year. Point to each one in order. Look at the picture of what is special about that month.

Calendar

January	February
March	April
May	June
July	August
September	October
November	December

Circle your favorite month. Write that month.

Answers will vary.

Draw an X next to your birthday month. Write that month.

Answers will vary.

Calendar

Draw a book next to the month you start school. Write that month.

Answers will vary.

BONUS: What is the first month of the year?

January

Now add this sticker to your map!

Trucks, Buses, and Trains

Compare each object.

Circle the **longer** train.

Circle the **taller** bus.

Circle the **heavier** dump truck.

Measuring

Duck. Duck!

One word can mean different things. Draw a line to match the pictures that share the same word.

Spelling and Vocabulary

Travel Time!

The cars and buses are parked at the airport.

Count as many cars and buses as you can aloud!

AIRPORT

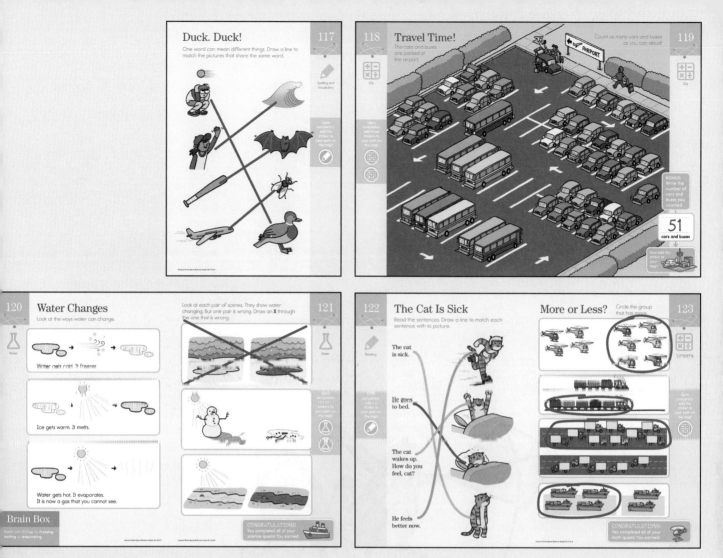

BONUS: Write the number of cars and buses you counted.

51 cars and buses

Now add this sticker to your map!

Water Changes

Look at the ways water can change.

Water

Water gets cold. It freezes.

Ice gets warm. It melts.

Water gets hot. It evaporates. It is now a gas that you cannot see.

Brain Box

Water can change by freezing, melting, or evaporating.

Look at each pair of scenes. They show water changing. But one pair is wrong. Draw an **X** through the one that is wrong.

Water

CONGRATULATIONS! You completed all of your science quests! You earned:

The Cat Is Sick

Read the sentences. Draw a line to match each sentence with its picture.

Reading

The cat is sick.

He goes to bed.

The cat wakes up. How do you feel, cat?

He feels better now.

More or Less?

Circle the group that has more.

Comparing

CONGRATULATIONS! You completed all of your math quests! You earned:

ABC You Later!

Uh-oh! Some of the letters in the alphabet have disappeared. Can you trace the dotted letters and write the missing ones?

ABC

Aa Bb Cc Dd
Ee Ff Gg Hh
Ii Jj Kk Ll Mm
Nn Oo Pp Qq
Rr Ss Tt Uu Vv
Ww Xx Yy Zz

CONGRATULATIONS! You completed all of your English language arts quests! You earned:

Summer Brain Quest Extras

Stay smart all summer long with these Summer Brain Quest Extras! In this section you'll find:

Summer Brain Quest Reading List

A book can take you anywhere— and summer is a great time to go on a reading adventure! Use the Summer Brain Quest Reading List to help you start the next chapter of your quest!

Summer Brain Quest Mini Deck

Cut out the cards and make your own Summer Brain Quest Mini Deck. Play by yourself or with a friend.

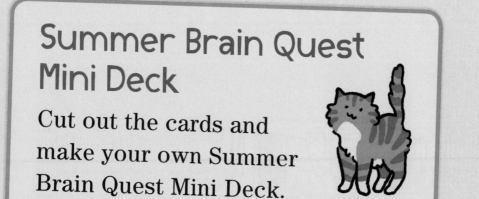

Summer Brain Quest Reading List

We recommend reading at least 15 to 30 minutes each day. Read to yourself or aloud. You can also read aloud with a friend or family member and discuss the book. Here are some questions to get you started:

- Was the book a nonfiction (informational) or fiction (story/narrative) text?

- Who or what was the book about?

- What was the setting of the story (where did it take place)?

- Was there a main character? Who was it? Describe the character.

- Was there a problem in the story? What was it? How was it solved?

- Were there any lessons in the book?

- Why do you think the author wrote the book?

Jump-start your reading adventure by visiting your local library or bookstore and checking out the following books. Track which ones you've read, and write your own review! Would you recommend this book to a friend? If so, which friend would you recommend this book to, and why?

Fiction

Anna Hibiscus, written by Atinuke, illustrated by Lauren Tobia

Anna lives in a city in West Africa, where she splashes on the beach, sells oranges, and plans a party. She lives with her extended family in a beautiful compound.

DATE STARTED: _____   DATE FINISHED: _____

MY REVIEW: _____

_____

Be Patient, Pandora!, written by Joan Holub, illustrated by Leslie Patricelli

Pandora's mother warns her not to open a box, but Pandora is just too curious. She tries touching it, then leaning on it, then, accidentally, it opens! The surprise inside is ruined. But there might still be something left to share with her mother.

DATE STARTED: _____   DATE FINISHED: _____

MY REVIEW: _____

_____

Big Red Lollipop, written by Rukhsana Khan, illustrated by Sophie Blackall

Rubina's mother makes Rubina take her little sister Sana to a birthday party. Then Sana eats both of their party favors! Later, when Sana is faced with a similar situation, sisterly love prevails.

DATE STARTED: _____   DATE FINISHED: _____

MY REVIEW: _____

_____

Brave Irene, written and illustrated by William Steig

Irene's mother has fallen ill. But the ball gown she has sewn must be delivered to a fancy ball tonight! Irene braves a blizzard to make the delivery, and the partygoers are amazed!

DATE STARTED: _____   DATE FINISHED: _____

MY REVIEW: _____

_____

Doctor Ted, written by Andrea Beaty, illustrated by Pascal Lemaitre

Ted's school really needs a doctor. So he decides to become one.

DATE STARTED: _____   DATE FINISHED: _____

MY REVIEW: _____

_____

Dex: The Heart of a Hero, written by Caralyn Buehner, illustrated by Mark Buehner

Little Dex the Dachshund works hard to become a superdog. But Cleevis the cat bullies Dex. When Cleevis needs help one day, Dex shows that he truly has the heart of a hero.

DATE STARTED: _____   DATE FINISHED: _____

MY REVIEW: _____

_____

The Gardener, written by Sarah Stewart, illustrated by David Small

During the Great Depression, a girl goes to stay with her uncle in the city. Slowly, she transforms the barren rooftop into a beautiful garden.

DATE STARTED: _____ DATE FINISHED: _____

MY REVIEW: _____

_____

Last Stop on Market Street, written by Matt de la Peña, illustrated by Christian Robinson

A boy learns to see beauty in the city around him during his weekly outing with his grandmother.

DATE STARTED: _____ DATE FINISHED: _____

MY REVIEW: _____

_____

My Lucky Day, written and illustrated by Keiko Kasza

When a pig knocks on Mr. Fox's door, the fox can't believe his luck. What a delicious treat! But wouldn't Pig be even more delicious if he were fattened up (with a big meal), tenderized (with a massage), and bathed? That's what Pig suggests, as he makes his own good luck.

DATE STARTED: _____ DATE FINISHED: _____

MY REVIEW: _____

_____

Our Animal Friends at Maple Hill Farm, written by Alice Provensen, illustrated by Martin Provensen

Maple Hill Farm has a lot of animal friends, each with their own distinct—and sometimes hilarious—personalities!

DATE STARTED: _____ DATE FINISHED: _____

MY REVIEW: _____

_____

Sleepless Knight, by James Sturm, Andrew Arnold, and Alexis Frederick-Frost

For her first camping trip, the Knight and her horse, Edward, pack all the things they need, including Teddy. When it's time for sleep, Teddy is nowhere to be found, and the quest is on to make everything just right before bedtime.

DATE STARTED: _____ DATE FINISHED: _____

MY REVIEW: _____

_____

Nonfiction

The Dinosaur Alphabet Book, written by Jerry Pallotta, illustrated by Ralph Masiello

There is a dinosaur for every letter of the alphabet! Learn about them all in this colorful picture book.

DATE STARTED: _____ DATE FINISHED: _____

MY REVIEW: _____

_____

Family Pictures/Cuadros de Familia, written and illustrated by Carmen Lomas Garza

In words and paintings, the artist recounts vivid memories of growing up in South Texas. The book is in English and Spanish.

DATE STARTED: _____ DATE FINISHED: _____

MY REVIEW: _____

_____

Home, written and illustrated by Carson Ellis

People live in a variety of homes. In stories, they may even live in a shoe! Children explore the concept of home in this artful and cozy book.

DATE STARTED: _____ DATE FINISHED: _____

MY REVIEW: _____

_____

A Little Book of Sloth, written and photographed by Lucy Cooke

Meet the baby sloths living in the largest sloth sanctuary in the world.

DATE STARTED: _____   DATE FINISHED: _____

MY REVIEW: _____

_____

Mama Miti: Wangari Maathai and the Trees of Kenya, written by Donna Jo Napoli, illustrated by Kadir Nelson

Learn how Nobel Prize winner Wangari Maathai helped her country and the world by planting trees.

DATE STARTED: _____   DATE FINISHED: _____

MY REVIEW: _____

_____

My First Day, written by Steve Jenkins, illustrated by Robin Page

What do baby animals do on the day they are born? It depends on the species. Learn about penguins, Siberian tigers, and more!

DATE STARTED: _____   DATE FINISHED: _____

MY REVIEW: _____

_____

Now and Ben, written and illustrated by Gene Barretta

Did you know Ben Franklin invented bifocals? Or that he had the idea for daylight saving time? See Ben's original inventions compared to how they look today.

DATE STARTED: _____   DATE FINISHED: _____

MY REVIEW: _____

_____

Raindrops Roll, written and photographed by April Pulley Sayre

Explore the wonder of rain and the water cycle in this photo-illustrated picture book.

DATE STARTED: _____   DATE FINISHED: _____

MY REVIEW: _____

_____

Rotten Pumpkin, written by David M. Schwartz, photographed by Dwight Kuhn

What happens when a pumpkin rots? A lot, actually. And in the end, it fosters the growth of an all-new pumpkin plant!

DATE STARTED: _____   DATE FINISHED: _____

MY REVIEW: _____

_____

We Dig Worms!, written and illustrated by Kevin McCloskey

An underground tour through the hidden world of earthworms answers the questions of what worms do all day, how they see, and why they're so squishy.

DATE STARTED: _____   DATE FINISHED: _____

MY REVIEW: _____

_____

What If You Had Animal Teeth, written by Sandra Markle, illustrated by Howard McWilliam

What if you had elephant teeth, or shark teeth, or the giant tooth of a narwhal? Learn about the toothy traits of these and other animals.

DATE STARTED: _____   DATE FINISHED: _____

MY REVIEW: _____

_____

And don't stop here! There's a whole world to discover. All you need is a book!

Summer Brain Quest Mini Deck

QUESTIONS

Are there more lemons or pickles?

Which of the 5 senses is missing?

QUESTIONS

Which word goes in the blank?

He _____ cold.

is   am   are

Which community worker keeps swimmers safe?

QUESTIONS

How many sides does this shape have?

SCHOOL CROSSING

Which one would you see in the fall?

QUESTIONS

Say the sound of the letter **r**. Which word begins with this letter?

Which one is the American flag?

ANSWERS

He **is** cold.

ANSWERS

lemons

touch

ANSWERS

rainbow

ANSWERS

5 sides

SCHOOL
CROSSING

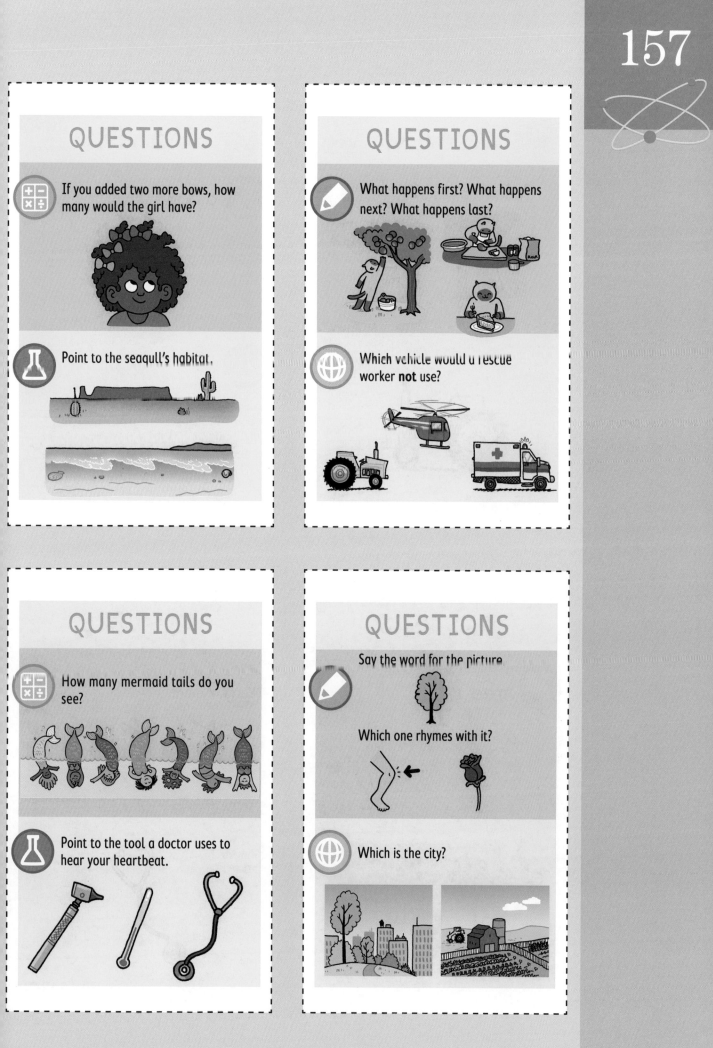

QUESTIONS

If you added two more bows, how many would the girl have?

Point to the seagull's habitat.

QUESTIONS

What happens first? What happens next? What happens last?

Which vehicle would a rescue worker **not** use?

QUESTIONS

How many mermaid tails do you see?

Point to the tool a doctor uses to hear your heartbeat.

QUESTIONS

Say the word for the picture.

Which one rhymes with it?

Which is the city?

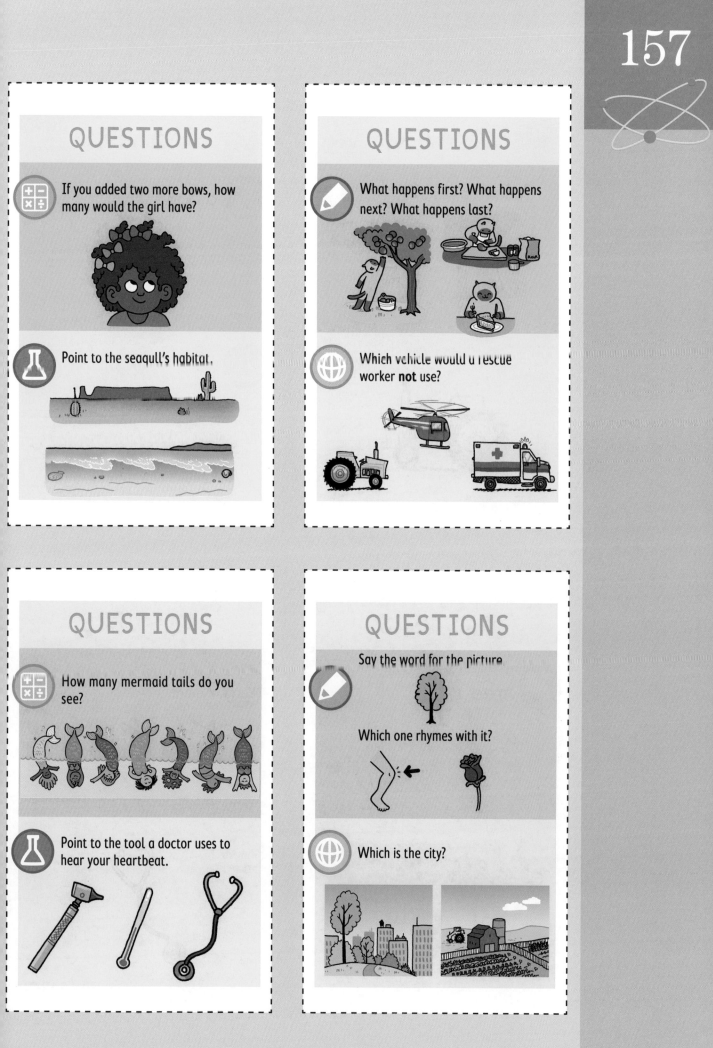

QUESTIONS

If you blew out 2 candles, how many would still be burning?

Wood comes from which natural resource?

QUESTIONS

Which letter should be an uppercase letter in this sentence?

she swims far.

Which is our national bird?

QUESTIONS

Which cone has the most scoops of ice cream?

What did the beavers build?

QUESTIONS

Say the word for the picture.

Which animal rhymes with the word?

Which sign means it is safe to walk?

WALK

DON'T WALK

ANSWERS

✏️ **S**he swims far.

🌐 bald eagle

ANSWERS

➕ 2 candles

🧪 tree

ANSWERS

✏️ mitten

kitten *mew*

🌐 WALK

ANSWERS

➕ 8 scoops

🧪

Level 1

START!

Level 2

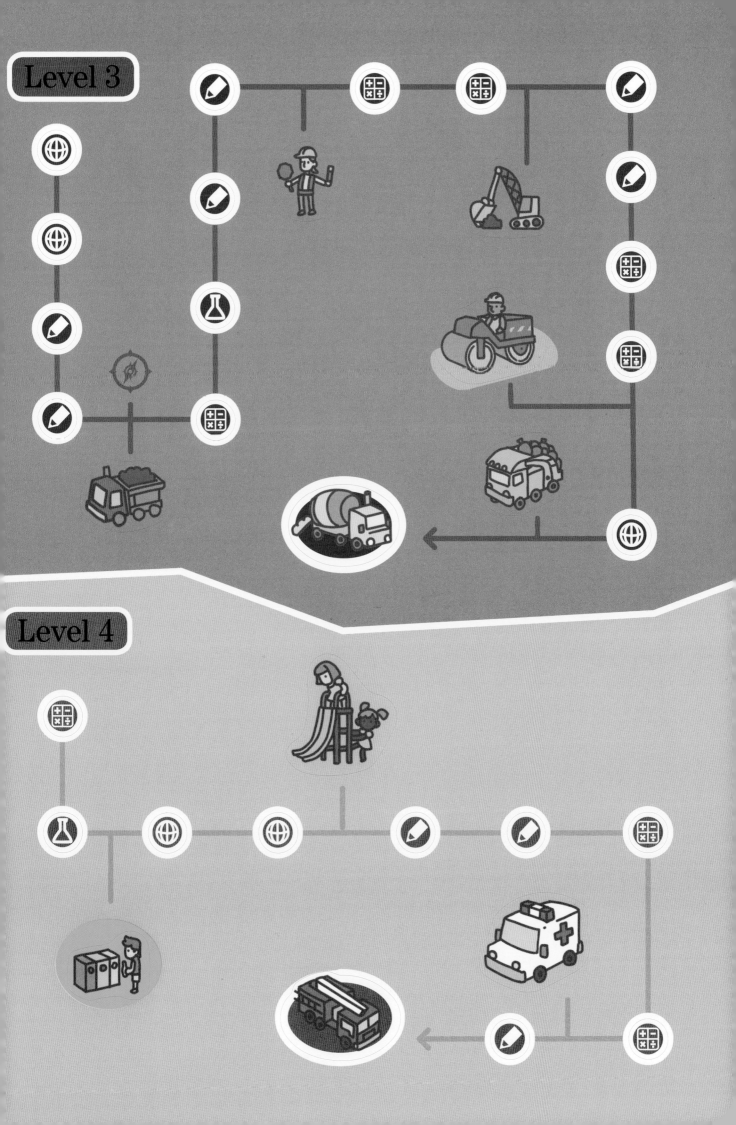

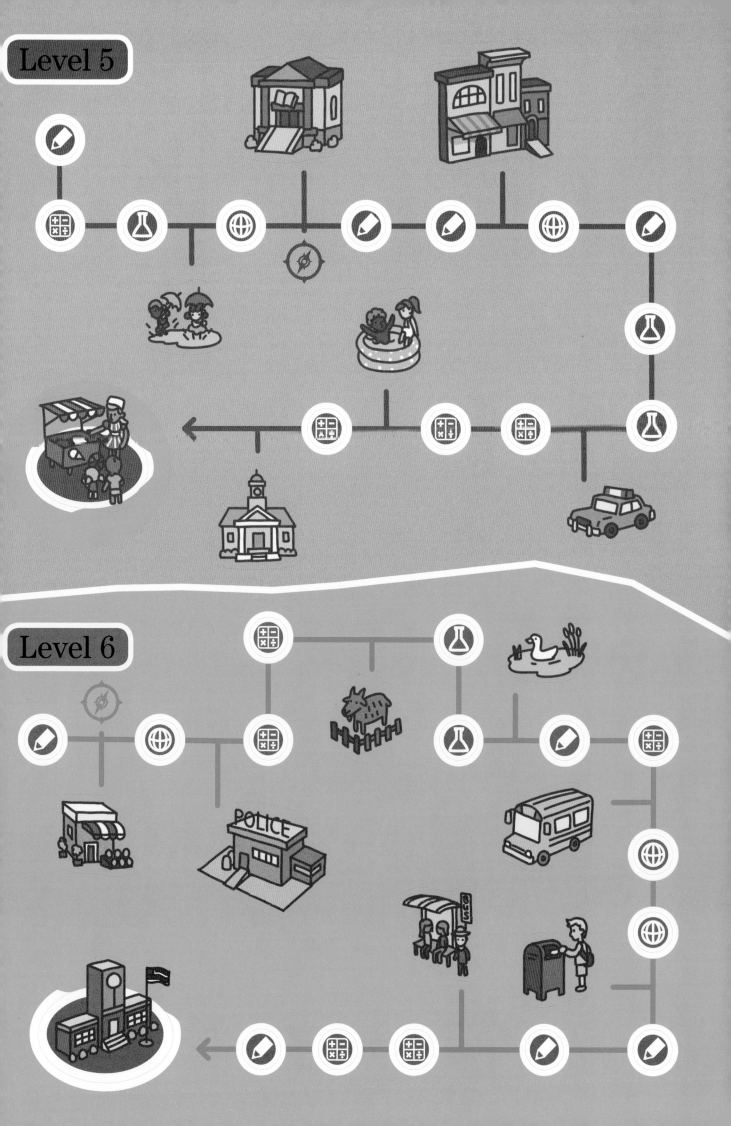

Level 5

Level 6

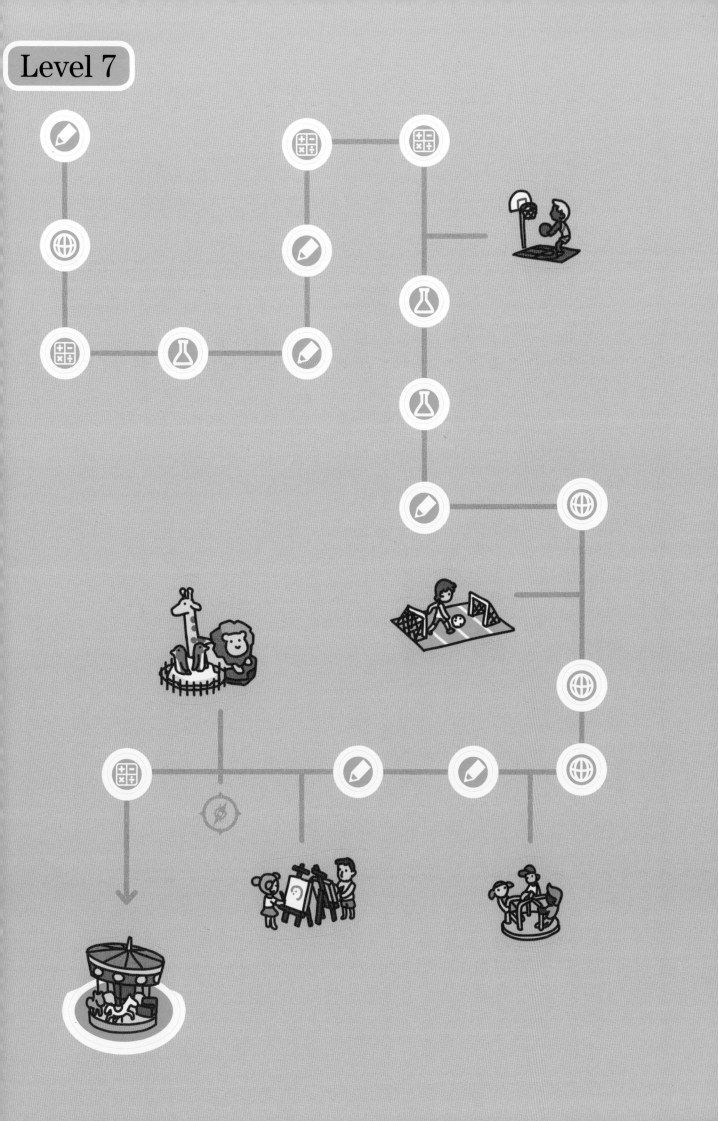

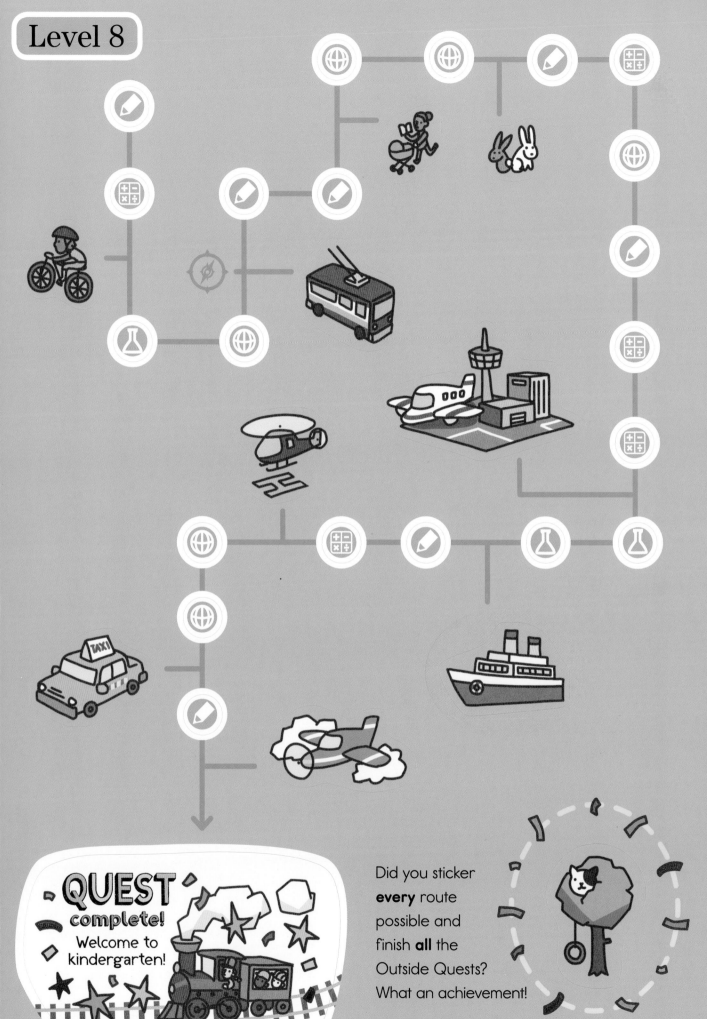

Level 8

QUEST complete!
Welcome to kindergarten!

Did you sticker **every** route possible and finish **all** the Outside Quests? What an achievement!

You've earned the
100% STICKER!